Awakening Fire

VERONICA VALLES

BALBOA®
PRESS
A DIVISION OF HAY HOUSE

Balboa Press books may be ordered through booksellers or by contacting:

Balboa Press
A Division of Hay House
1663 Liberty Drive
Bloomington, IN 47403
www.balboapress.com
1 (877) 407-4847

ISBN: 978-1-5043-3005-3 (sc)
ISBN: 978-1-5043-3006-0 (e)

Library of Congress Control Number: 2015904495

Print information available on the last page.

Balboa Press rev. date: 4/15/2015

Contents

Introduction

To be real honest, I'm not sure how it all got started. I remember reading a journal piece I wrote, "It's my story...and I'm not sticking to it" for one of Robin Hackett's CD releases at the Center for Spiritual Living, Dallas. A year later, I wrote "Enlightened Duality" and performed it with Charity Lankford in the 2007 talent show.

I had written many final projects for spiritual classes at the Center and my emails over the years are testaments to my growth and expansion utilizing the principles of Science of Mind as well as my dance with the Divine. The poetry began to flow and each invitation to write I saw how I was immersed in silent chords of doubt and denial which transmuted into a resounding YES as I surrendered it to the Greater Writer, God, the Divine within, the spark of creativity that writes as me. I began to realize I had the gift of being a word-weaver to share, a light to unleash and that it was SPIRIT in, through and AS me.

The very fact I have never considered myself a poet is what is so amusing about it all. I am just a passionate witness to the beauty of life and complexities of being. I dance in delight and write, write, write. I bear witness to the multidimensional experiences of being SPIRIT in my sweet human form, savoring it all.…the tears, fears, joys, exuberant recognitions that it is ALL GOD. I have over 7,000 pages of writings thanks to Julia Cameron's *The Artist Way* Morning Pages. Dreams, fears, successes, loves, losses, poems and more etched and sketched my day.

My vision and mission as an artist is to inspire you to awaken to your FIRE...the Light that is your life expressing. To find the passion in being, the treasures in the simplest of gifts, and to truly cherish your human form knowing it is SPIRIT weaving in, through and AS you. I am here to open hearts to LOVE.

Many of the pieces were written for specific events at the Center for Spiritual Living, Dallas, a New Thought community, as well as other local, collaborative events. These are the classic pieces of the past before I went into Ministerial School for four years that took of my time, energy and expression. I also added a few additional writings – a post from the Shirley Maclaine site where I was "MysticHeart," (prior to that, "A Seeker"), an email I sent to my friends called, "SkyPainter," as well as little hellos from 2007. Somewhere in my files are hundreds of haikus written during that time period. Musings pour forth and lay around in books, boxes, airline napkins and storage units. Wrapped in memory are moments of my life.

Spoken word-poetry has a cadence, a rhythmic measure that is not transferrable from the author to the listener in published form. The energy I radiate from the stage too is not present yet the light laces every word with Love. So it is what it IS. Let it ignite your spirit and inspire you into greater seeing and being. Take the word as a light pill...let it be your charge to shine your JOY in the world and radiate LOVE everywhere you go.

In deep gratitude and deeper LOVE,
Veronica Valles

1. Kissing God

Did you know....
when you inhale
then exhale
the perfume of each moment
you are kissing GOD.

Did you know...
that when you smile at a stranger
wave as if you have reunited
with your long lost friend
you are kissing GOD.

Did you know...
that every time
you sink into the sunset
or swim in your lover's arms
you are kissing GOD.

Did you know....
that when you look
in the mirror
and wink at your LIGHT
you are kissing GOD.

Did you know...
that every tear wiped from a child's eye
every fever you healed
with your LOVE
you are kissing GOD.

Did you know...
how beautiful LIFE IS
how precious each soul
dancing in delight
IS always kissing GOD.

Go out and kiss GOD tonight...
a thousand times.
Melt into the Beloved's lips of LIGHT
and Illuminate the world
one kiss at a time.

2.23.06

2. EnLightened Duality

Voice of GREAT DOUBT -- Part 1

I lie naked on the floor
lost in the darkness of delusion
tricksters of my mind
taunting me
loneliness strangling my LIGHT
as I gasp for any semblance of TRUTH   **I never knew there was a VOID**
never heard of such an empty existence
a rumor once circling
between whispers of doubt
amongst the walking dead   **I'm so confused**
yet someone told me
as if hexing me with a curse
of such vast emptiness
leading me to the distilled waters
cocktails that altered my consciousness
deeper into confusion
leading me astray
from my CREATIVE GENIUS   **Brilliant, aren't I?**
lost in a labyrinth of lies
twisted deceit
a fragile psyche
a wounded ego
a lost soul
life missing in action
frustration forged my path
sinking into the quick sand
distortions
of vapid guests
masquerading as lurking shadows
disguised as friends
who hid behind liquid courage
luring me with their charm

      **half ass attempts of
enlightened duality**

withering away
into that nothingness   **(pause)... I don't feel anything**

Peer pressure
shoved me into submission
relinquishing my heart and dreams
cowering in the corner
naked in my opinions that only the dust would attend
the VOID   **I never knew there was such a VOID**
it haunted me   **I never knew there was such a VOID**
hollow cries of creativity suffocated
extreme sadness
exaggerated madness
was this all my humanness
could derive   **Is this IT?**
Could there be such a cruel Master
who created only life
one disaster at a time

                                      What is so wonderful
                                      about such pain?

wreaking in irreverence
assaulting all that is GOOD
by acting out
insulting impulses of
what adults suppress
how did I inherit
such animosity
towards my TRUTH   **What is the TRUTH?**
why are the innocents
draped in negative language   **What innocence?**
that denigrates   **I've lost my innocence.**
suffocates
masturbates
moronic excuses
of self absorption
distortion
divorced from SOURCE
not knowing

what to do
who to be
where to go
never feeling quite at home
Late night wanderings
within the dark alleys
of my scarred mind
wrapped in stories
of someone else's
false perceptions
negative projections
beauty belittled
dreams raped of their imagination
LIGHT diluted with drama
slipping deeper into amnesia
a hurricane of emotions
uncontained fire
whose fury
burned my very existence
into ashes

Ruts became routine
excuses became my mantras

I looked in the mirror
no one was there
darkness creeped
into every crevice
of my being
emptiness oozed from my
dehydrated soul
my ego was smothered
with the soot of ignorance
I screamed for someone
or something
greater than me
larger than my mind
more powerful than pain

What do I do?
Who the hell am I? ..(pause 4 seconds)

Where do I belong?

I don't know anything
How do I keep up

I never knew there was such a VOID.

supplicating sorrows
tears flooding a thousand oceans
beseeching the unknown
on my knees
wailing in the
Why? Why? Why?

**Why did you create me? Why is there so much pain?
Why don't you do something about it?**

Aren't you the Almighty?

I assaulted the ONE
with insinuations
of a dead-beat father   **You're not fair?**
belittling life
as a rag doll existence
pandering to the lies
who stole my LIGHT
wanting to be rescued…resuscitated
resurrected
into my GLORY
that lurked
in the sweetness
of my childhood

when magic was real   **It was so real**
and I could fly   **I could really fly**
with the snap
of my little fingers
Here I lay
drowning in tears
drained of my lifeforce   **Sigh**
disbelief as my compass   **So, why am I here? Do you even care? Why don't you**
to even darker days   **take it away or do something about it. I guess I was**
call of the weary   **just born this way. I can't feel this way anymore.**
chants of confusion   **What if I never change? Oh, my GOD, will I ever**
WHY? WHY? WHY?   **change?**

Voice of GOD--Part 2

In the stillness of such sorrow
I surrendered to my innocence
I remembered as a child
a LIGHT so BRIGHT
a LOVE so
STRONG
a LIFE so PURE
invoking the ONE
I cried, so softly
"Please...show me where you are and show me who I am."

Oh Sweet Child
of the UNIVERSE
I AM Right HERE, right NOW
The POWER and the PRESENCE
LIGHT shapeshifted
into form
Life in, around
As and through you

Luminosity stirred within me
invited me
into the fullness
of my being
I asked out loud,
"Who are you?"

I AM the ONE
Hymns of my being
sing as ALL
I AM the dance of heaven and earth

Of the billions of suns
I AM the inexhaustible SOURCE
Of the myriad bodies
I AM each precious form
Of the INFINITE fields of possibilities

I AM the seeds
Of the countless manifestations
I am born of each dream
I AM the silence
in between the gap
I AM the glimmer of TRUTH
in between the doubt
I AM the PEACE
in the stillness of the cause
I AM the immutable
molding life through every thought
I AM the sweetness of HARMONY　　　　　　(sings) HARMONY
in the midst of bitter chaos

ONE MIND　　　　　　　　　　　　　　　ONE MIND
made manifest
in a million names
ONE LOVE　　　　　　　　　　　　　　　ONE LOVE
expressing
in INFINTE ways
Involution……Evolution
CREATIVE GENIUS
at play

Truth Revealed -- Part 3

As my TRUTH
began to emerge
impurities
of my mind
filtered
through the LIGHT
Unconditional LOVE
baptized my
sweet little ego
gently stirring me
into awakening
as I was remembering
who I am

Then SPIRIT spoke to me—
Oh precious child of GOD
YOU are LOVE incarnate
Liquid sundrop
of exquisite BEAUTY
My LIFE
is your LIFE
Precious Patterns
of perfection
flowing as you
through you
DIVINE PRINCIPLE
key to the kingdom
within
TRUTH your touchstone
WISDOM your guide
JOY your compass
HARMONY your heartbeat

If I am all that then what is this emptiness that I have felt for so long? What is the VOID?

Sacred emptiness
is your canvas

INFINITE playing field
of possibilities
the VOID
the space
of pregnant potentiality
seeded with prayer
your MIND
the MASTER of
every desire
tapping into
Universal MIND
moving molecules
into manifestation

So what is fear?
FEAR
the four
lettered
word
your sweet little ego
latches onto
to play small
for indeed
your MAGNIFICENCE
is waiting
to emerge
from the cocoon
of hibernation
stand in your
immovable center
within
as you watch
fear dissolve
into TRUTH

What do I do with FREE will? Isn't this your GIFT to me?
What?

Use it.
Yea, use it.
It's the Gift

to yourself
DIVINE plan
is FREEDOM
to BE   **Freedom?**
simply BE
all you wish
to experience and
express
with your choices   **Choices?**
LAW creating
through every
action
reaction
distraction
all your CHOICE   **My Choice?**
as you conceive
believe
receive
all your CHOICE   **My choice??**
What you embody
embrace
emanate
Let me
remind you
ALL YOUR CHOICE   **Oh, MY Choice**
destructive or constructive
pleasure or pain
love or anger
you CHOOSE

harmony or hatred   **(sings) HARMONY**
drama queen or centered being
ecstasy or madness
YOU CHOOSE
be led by
illuminated
inner guide
or a pack of

half lit
blind beggars
YOU CHOOSE   **Hey, hey…take it easy**
dance in
BELOVED's delight   **I can dance**
or partake
in the communion
of commiseration
YOU CHOOSE

demons in drag
friends on the rag
souls on fire
joyful desire
YOU CHOOSE
Door #1
Door #2
Door #3
Window #4
YOU CHOOSE   **I CHOOSE**

Stand in your POWER
melt as a coward
Freedom or bondage
YOU CHOOSE   **I CHOOSE**
Do you SEE now?
Do you get it?
Are you awake yet?   **I AM Awake**

So simple…just BE…

BE PEACE
BE JOY
BE HARMONY   **(sings) HARMONY**
BE LOVE

Standing in the TRUTH -- Part 4

I now stand in the TRUTH
of my being
illuminated by the inner fire
DIVINE MIND is my mind   **Yes, it is**
never knew I co-create my LIFE
by aligning
with the PRESENCE
never knew I could be
emancipated
by remembering the POWER   **It is yours.**
of my ESSENCE
now dancing in reverence
praising all that is GOOD   **YES!**
reveling in my MAGNIFICENCE   **You are MAGNIFICENT**
glory of ten thousand suns
PEACE of the ONE
drumming as my heart   **PEACE**
fury of my MIND
transmuted into FIRE of FAITH   **Your true POWER**
contradictions deciphered
infusion of GRACE   **YES!**
Healing water
of realization
quenched my
dehydrated soul   **TRUTH**
dreams resuscitated
from submission
breath of the ONE   **Breathe**
LIFE draped in deliciousness
thoughts that create
living
laughing
loving
aware and awake
blurred vision
restored to CLARITY

guiding me HOME   **To your LOVE**
sanctified
glorified
purified
resurrection
of my soul   **YES!**
No one to
shame or blame
No one
to insult or assault
No one
to belittle or betray
No more playing small

VOICE of GREAT DOUBT
difused by DIVINE WISDOM
VOICE of GOD
illuminating my DIVINITY

NOW I know
truly know
GOD is my SOURCE
dancing in the fire of
creation
and joyful BLISS

I AM PEACE
I AM the TRUTH
I AM HARMONY
I AM SPIRIT   **MOVE into chant You Are LOVE**

2007

3. Awakening Fire

Turn on the 6 o'clock news
World is seemingly on fire
Chaos of complexity
Paradigms of pain
Screeching out as war
Of all sorts
Constipation of complaints
Choir of ego refrains
Imposing illusion
In the suburbs of our mind
Degradation of the Garden of Paradise
Cut throat comments that strangle the soul
Beautiful round world
Constrained with imaginary straight lines
Rigid rules and regulation
creating jagged borders of separation
Severing the hearts of humanity
Dissecting the SOURCE of our divinity
Swords of ignorance
Defiling our innocence
Brother fighting against brother
Sister assaulting sister
Children orphaned of their imagination
Suicidal annihilation
Ghost machines sauntering in the world
Spewing psychic pollution
Stunting evolution
Deceiving into believing
That this darkness called violence
Self imposed exile from LOVE
That this perversion of power
Can destroy the ONE

Despite the high rise of excuses
Story built upon story
Babel tower of delusion
Despite the games of denigration
False indoctrination
Media moguls manipulation
Despite the clashes of cultural conditioning
Tug of wars of indifference
Forked tongues of deliverance
Despite seeming fragmentation
Inflammatory accusations
Millennium of lies perpetuated

I am not deterred by this parade of foolishness
Confused confessions of duality
Us vs. other diatribes
Instead, I turn ON to TRUTH
Dancing with the Indwelling PRESENCE
Playing in fields of INFINITE POSSIBILITIES
I declare the ONENESS of BEING
Overriding raucous clamoring of conditioning
I circle the sacred mountain of GREATNESS
With pristine awareness
Seeing WHOLENESS in creation
I stand witness to the BEAUTY of the DIVINE
In every delicious incarnation
Ignoring incantations of separation
I open my heart to the FIRE of UNCONDITIONAL LOVE
Freely Giving and Receiving
Attending to the ONE in the many
Wiping clear the muddied mind
Stained by institutional deception
Shamelessly blamed on Adam and Eve

I stand here in this TRUTH and only TRUTH

To the secrets revealed to me

By the whispers of the ONE

Indeed you and I

Are seeds of a supernova

Whose exquisite LIGHT cannot be

Contained or

Restrained

You and I

Are the dance of the BELOVED

Tango of light and shadow

Bejeweled in splendor and wonder

You and I

Are warriors of LOVE

Unleashed fire of CREATION

Transmuting poison into medicine

You and I

Are the wisdomkeepers

Spiritual peacemakers

Protectors of innocence

Declarers of our MAGNIFICENCE

You and I

Are woven from AGAPE

Cloth of many colors

UNDERSTANDING wrapped in

Buddhas and lovers

You and I

Are the kingdom of Christ consciousness

Wildmind of realization

Pristine CLARITY of illumination

You and I

Are gorgeous blooms

In the garden of Paradise

Offered to the world in a bouquet of blessings

You and I
Are indeed ONE
Dance of GOD upon GOD
LOVE upon LOVE
LIGHT upon LIGHT

It is in this TRUTH
I can no longer attend your small stories
I attend only to your glorious nature
It is in this TRUTH
I can no longer attend your false pretenses
I attend only to your LOVE and MAGNIFICENCE
It is in this TRUTH
I can no longer attend your strangulation of LIGHT
I attend only to your pristine AWARENESS
It is in this TRUTH
I can no longer attend your resistance
I attend only to your STRENGTH & COURAGE
It is in this TRUTH
I can no longer attend your illusion
I attend only to your BEAUTY & JOY

It is in this TRUTH
The FIRE of AWAKENING
Ignites a supernova of ABSOLUTE LOVE
Creating a new paradigm

It is in this TRUTH
In which PEACE is born within
God seeds nourished into being
Enveloping the world in LIGHT

It is in this TRUTH I DANCE with you
The POWER of the ONE
Sacred Celebration
64 Daily Revelations of this Season

It is in this TRUTH
I live, move, breathe and have my being
Immersed in the PRESENCE
Savoring each ESSENCE

It is in this TRUTH I LOVE.

Season for Nonviolence Opening Ceremony CSL Dallas 1.30.08

4. Beloved Community

"Beloved Community"
We celebrate with millions
This sacred journey HOME
64 days
Simple ways
To remember
we are ONE

'Our life is our message'
Unveiled in an unspoken promise of GOOD
Derivatives of LOVE
Pulsating as LIFE
Revealing the "united proclamation" that
"nothing lives in this world but TRUTH"

Mingling voices
Of Gandhi, King and Chavez
wisdom teachings
Of countless others
Cultivating a new society
This DIVINE sobriety
Awakening each of us
To BE the difference
We wish to SEE
In the world

A simple SMILE recognizing
the POWER and PRESENCE in another
childlike innocence dissolves any barriers
A COURAGEous stance
For TRUTH in the midst of indifference

Illuminates deception
Beginning WITHIN
Extending in every direction
DREAMING in the immanence
Of a peaceful world
More powerful than war
in BELIEVING in the infallibility that
"YES, it is possible"

You SEE...This journey
Is a call to LOVE
a call to PLAY
A call to GOD
In every way

Words carry us forward
"insistence on TRUTH"
Was Gandhi's premise
In this "silent sense" of our DIVINE REALITY
We can no longer incite ignorance
With such pristine tools of deliverance
No more games of separation
As we see GOD in every emanation
Advances of new, creative solutions
Is a simple COMMITMENT
to the INTEGRITY of our conscience
Which creates consequences that
Can preserve this PRECIOUS planet

We cannot arrive at PEACE
Tripping over a pair of opposites
We can arrive
At the point of a New Earth
From an elevated state

21

UNDERSTANDING underlying
The DIVINE as it moves, breathes as ALL LIFE

Beloved Community
I SEE PEACE
In all of her GLORY
I have been to the mountaintop
Mesmerized by the gifts
Of splendor and wonder
I am a whirling dervish of LOVE
In the sweetness of my desire
To awaken each of you
To this mystical FIRE
I see INFINITY in your eyes
DIVINITY as the song of your being
In this space
PEACE is seeded
In this place
LOVE reforms
In this dance
BEAUTY I behold

For I KNOW this to be TRUE....

Above division
Above derision
Above confusion
Lives this VISION

So....let me ask YOU....

Can you walk the talk
Beyond the Season
Can you inspire, organize

Add rhyme and reason
To a different way of being
Outside the realm
Of blind conformity
Will you persist in ACCOUNTABILITY
Moving through seeming conflict
With INTEGRITY

Can you see beyond dualistic illusion
OPENNESS and GRACIOUS to
The infusion
Of ideas and people
Tearing down fences
Disarming false accusations
Of instigated Race consciousness
Are you ready
To experience the larger context
Participating in this spiritual revolution

Can you hear the TRUTH
In the murmurs of an inarticulate culture
Where violence is disguised as entertainment
"less than" often nurtured
Will you add your voice into the void
Healing the soul segregation
With every directed intention
Centered in nonviolence
Instilling the sacred

Will you lend your heart, your hands, your time
In conscious acts of SERVICE
GIVING GRACE stimulated by LOVE
For your brothers and sisters
Will you insist on EQUALITY and worldwide CIVILITY

Will you stand in the power of purchase
Disavowing corporate gluttons
Guilty of societal degradation

Will you make the world a better place
By beginning with the BELOVED's embrace
Amongst friends you haven't met
Disguised as strangers
Reveling in their UNIQUENESS
Unconditionally bringing LIGHT
Into the corners of their day
Where shadows lurk
Pretending to be a danger

Will you offer the treasure of your heart
The gift of your being
Opening dialogues at your home and work
Dissolving walls of prejudice and aggression
Even subtle forms of annihilation
Such as gossip and judgment

Will you take a stance detached from
False ego..........False pride
False strength........False bravado
In the name of DISARMAMENT

Will you add laughter in the mix of seriousness
Will you illuminate MINDFULLY the mysterious
Will you be a BENEFICIAL PRESENCE
mandala of COMPASSION
In every circumstance
Will you charm conditions with
Your thoughts, words and volition
Will you celebrate LIFE's preciousness

Savoring all that is delicious
Not distracted by
The media's stereotypical infilitration

You have answered this invitation to PEACE
You have planted in the Garden of GOD
64 seeds
We celebrate where we have come
But where will you go tomorrow
Can you carry the VISION, celebrate the UNITY
Will you take the rose of your being
Perfuming reality with a deeper meaning

To Know GOD
Is to KNOW PEACE
To Know GOD
Is to BE LOVE
This is the FIRE which
Ignites a planetary evolution
ADVOCACY of right ACTION
The power of the human SPIRIT
Free from Retribution
To triumph where dignity and worth prevail
Where every human is revered
As the individualized
Personified
Glorified
Face of the ONE

In this alchemy of music, dance, dialogue and more
Answer this call to ACTION
This Call to LOVE
As we transport beyond imagining
a world as ONE

In this sacred celebration
We have laid claim
To a new Kingdom
Right here it is done

ONLY if you remember tomorrow............What you carry today
ONLY if your devotion to PEACE...... Remains steadfast
To the wonder in which we play
ONLY if you join each other in the chants
Of the nameless ONE
Together we will grow
A fabulous new world
For all the children to COME.

Season for Peace and Nonviolence, Closing Ceremony,
Center for Spiritual Living Dallas, April 2008

5. Troubador

I'm a troubadour
Who looted heaven
For some sacred lyrics
Brought to earth as medicine
Jade jewels of remembering
I've come here to seed
Awakening each of you
To your DIVINITY

I am a fool like Hafiz
My heart dances naked in the streets
I am a glutton for experience
Savoring God's tantalizing feast
I joyfully
Gleefully
Jump off the edge
Of the little "r" of reality
Diving deeply into the river of YES

Heart open wide
Mind uncensored
I create delicious adventures
Skirting around disasters
I'm a paradigm buster
A paradox master
Globe wandering junkie
Driving life a little faster

I've crisscrossed the universe
In magic carpet rides
Rainbow colored crayons

Have painted my skies

I've swallowed the sun

Chased the luscious Moon

I've laughed galaxies into being

Been stupid drunk on my lover's perfume

I've held vigils with my friends

To the testament of their LIGHT

I've melted into the wildflower fields embrace

during my soul's dark night

I'm a maker of meaning

playing in kaleidoscope possibilities

Script my world into being

As I ignore

the doldrums of conformity

in this repertoire of GOD

my mission in life

is to call you to the wild

to stoke that inner fire

First kiss of the DIVINE

Sent me on this intoxicating fall

Swirling like a Sufi mystic

Enchanted with all

In childlike simplicity

Imbued with LOVE and GLORY

I see beyond your delusions

I'm not convinced of your little stories

Fire of supernova

Runs through our veins

Secrets of the cosmos

Echo our HOLY NAME

JOY ignites me as this passionate presence

As I incinerate your illusions
Revealing your EXQUISITE essence

For I see GOD in YOU
GOD in ME
I see GOD playing throughout INFINITY
The mirror I raise
Is to heal your dementia
Wiping clear the muddied mind
Which has inhibited your ascension
For the GLORY of the ONE
Is the GLORY of YOU
I'm a persistent, prickly visionary
In this pursuit of TRUTH

LOVE is the reason we have come into form
Nature's boldest challenge
Is to cultivate this koan
The hymn of your soul
Is the force of your being
It is the pulsation of your fire
Rhythmic measure of your melody
LOVE is bigger than death or any pain
It is the source of your bliss
Silencing the heckling of ego refrains
It is the altar we praise
In each other's essence
Heart to heart understanding
Source of our transcendence

These little aphorisms I tithe to you
A remembrance of the delicacy of the DIVINE
shining through

I have come here to play
I can't contain this FIRE
I'm only your mirror
Of SPIRIT's outpouring desire
When I watch you play small
Sinking in the quicksand of duality
See you stumble in the illusion of the lower reality
I just want to scream, HEY over here
So you can awaken and set yourself free

I look at you and marvel at your GLORY
I've fallen in love with your wonder not your story
I'm not a soothsayer, I am definitely not a savior
I'm just here to remind you
Of the liquid lucidity of your unique flavor

Imagine if the aurora borealis decided not to dance
Their emerald hallelujahs denied from our glance

Imagine if the hummingbird decided not to fly
Posing as rigor mortis instead of swinging in ruby delight

Imagine if the fireflies contained their fluorescent joy
Denying me the charm of this heavenly toy

Imagine if the sun suddenly lost its succulence
Tucked itself quietly at night without marmalade magnificence

Imagine if the magnolia withheld her seductive scent
Masked her sensuality with such irreverence

It's unimaginable to me
To see you hiding from your brilliance
It's unimaginable to me

Such adultery of your essence
It's unimaginable to me
That you are blinded from your GLORY
So I stand here in defiance ....Of those belittling stories

I made a promise
To the HOLY ONE
When I looted those lyrics
To daily remind you
That YOU...ARE....LOVE

Yes, I am a troubadour
A charmer of LIFE
I'll cheer in your BEAUTY
I'll bask in your LIGHT
My commitment to you
Strung along constellations
Is to mirror your MAGNIFICENCE
While I honor your journey's realizations
Waiting for you to see
What I see

Come play with me
In this River of YES
Knowing so richly
The DIVINE you express
Come play with me
In the wonders of this world
For I have fallen in love so deeply
With the BELOVED everywhere

I invite you..
To live lusciously
Deliciously

Juicy

I invite you to taste the mystery

I invite you to see beyond the small "r" of reality

I invite you....to LOVE

6. Cascading Colors of You

Two universes merged in Love
sparking a riot of delight
Divine filaments encoded as your genius
Shapeshifted into precious form
The Mystery emerged
Spray painting a luscious world
in cascading colors of YOU
Lavender lovesongs
along with cherry kissed sunsets
swirled and twirled in excitement
celebrating YOUR entrance
into earth's playingfield
galaxies cheered at life's bodaciousness
expressing as YOUR wonder
while the wind joined the party
in resounding hallelujahs
grateful for the simple TRUTH
of your sweet incarnation…for..
no other plays as you
no other can do what you do
one light adding to the greater glory
THIS is the reason YOU were born

Each of us comes into this world with a bundle
Talents wrapped in prayer silk shawls
Offered to others
In the name of the Holy One
Draping days and nights with wisdom and splendor
Intoxicating jasmine and plumeria
perfumes the path of the Garden of Paradise
pure fragrance of awakening

gentle rain of TRUTH upon a parched soul
fully blossoms seeds born of remembering
Magnificence glancing beyond the closed door of conformity
Unleashes a FIRE so potent
Freeing each of us to be
….exactly who we ARE.

I see that you are GOD dancing in exquisite form
Making a difference in each other's realms
Unique gifts that guide, share and direct the Light
Radiant transfiguration of the lower mind

A path of ten thousand tears and ten million smiles
Is this precious earth journey
Connected together in ONE heart

You are an elixir quenching dehydrated doubts
Who have forgotten the Source of their genuine power
Your laughter is healing music for a saddened soul
Compassionate recognition reminds each other we are whole
Like a cool breeze on a sultry summer day
Your presences soothes fear and anger
transmuting it into prayer with ease and grace
As you cartwheel through conditions in the joyfulness of a child
Seeing beyond illusion you cherish the journey of each mile
The Presence as your essence
Etches beauty across the landscapes of ONE mind
Leaving lovenote reminders in the pockets of mankind
Within our idiosyncrasies and prickly particularities
God plays in Infinite ways deliciously as each of us

One idea can spark a conscious revolution
One hug can heal any fear of separation
One ounce of encouragement can inspire a dreamer

One handshake hello invites home a seeming stranger

One open door for an elder bestows respect

One moment of support soothes solace and dispels distress.

One poem of fire breaks open a painfully sealed heart

One river feeds lavishly many fields near and far.

When you recognize your gifts

As the beautiful face of GOD

You unravel the layers of light

Driving through the seeming dark roads of duality

Together we move the earth around the sun

Unlimited power of love's visibility

Expresses as each one

Aware that you affect the world

With your song

Authentic call of greatness

Sets this world on FIRE

Lives touch upon lives, writing stories of meaning

Truth lives within truth, removing veils of ignorance

GOD expresses so succulently in wondrous perfection

We are here to mirror

the brilliance of being tangible constellations

Artisans of the Way

Let God out of the bag

Whirling like a dervish

Crazy in Love

Cascading colors of YOU

Paint this world in BEAUTY

Be it Do it …..all together…. we unleash our glory

11.23.08

7. New Year's Day Trilogy

Yesterday

Nothing exists beyond the now

not even the winds that eroded the edges of yesterday

can claim any power in this moment

yet pain persists provoked by

arguments of ancient hungry ghosts

whose murmurs of remorse

reverberate throughout my being

echoing refrains of missed opportunities, misguided heart and mind

a servant to regrets and self-inflicted criticisms

as bitter resentments

dilute my light

obscures the path of today

and conceals the trail to tomorrow

distracted by the obstacles

along my way

So I must call them forth

the pain, the wounds, the what ifs, should of, could of, would ofs..

these shackles of struggle

so I may release them from their seeming Samsonite grip

which has subdued me into submission

I must call them forth

As I shed light on the circumstances

Whose vignettes replay

in lingering disappointments

laced in my daily dialogues

I must call them forth

To illuminate them, these shadow dancers

These earthly dwellers, for the soul knows
The deeper TRUTH even
as light gets draped in tinges of sadness and sorrows

I honor that pain is real, palpable
yet it lives
not here in this present realm
this HOLY NOW
but in the corridors of the past
who have taken residence in crevices of my mind

I must call them forth
To bear witness
To the suffering caused
Suffering experienced
Suffering that must cease
I must call them forth
To bear witness
To the dilapidated dreams
A house divided
Broken promises whose jagged edges scar my heart

I must call them forth
subtle judgments, constricting labels, patterns to dissolve
That have frozen my mind
Jaded my truth
into this fire…I release all that no longer serves me

I call them forth
To bear witness
To my humanity
Lay claim to my divinity
as these relics of yesterday
That have contained me

Restrained me
are unleashed into the dancing dragon's den
transmuting them
Into pearls of wisdom
For there is no clinging
In the vastness of the INFINITE sky

I call forth…….liberating compassion….unconditional love….
breaking my heart wide open to receive LIGHT again

For in suffering….healing arises…penetrating beyond the horizon of yesterday…the
TRUTH of my essence mindfully brings me to today….as I release….and let go

So I call LOVE forth
As I travel forward
Restoring balance
evoking forgiveness
Uncovering Hidden gifts which
Awaken me to wholeness
Offering my tears to heaven
So they may rain upon the earth

…I call LOVE forth…..as I surrender my yesterday to the DIVINE today…

I release….I let go….I release…I let go…I release…

Today

Simple gaze

Within

Reveals

Potency

Of your

Light

Give your heart

To Love

Today

.... here

.... Now

Pure

Spacious

Open mind

Reveals vastness

Of TRUTH

See

As GOD

Sees

Standing

In this

Moment

Lucid.

Claim

your Holy Elixir

The

I AM.

Taste

Freedom

Which is yours

To Be

Be Love
Be JOY
Be WHOLE
So perfect
Right here

Standing at the doorway
A new path
Emerges
Move forward
In TRUTH
In Love
Inhale
Exhale
In the
holy pause
Before the
next step
In FAITH
In TRUST
Today
All is well
All is LOVE
All is GOD
There is only LOVE
Only.......LOVE

Celebration

Come….come dance
To this wild love poem
You have written to the GOD within

Ten thousand lyrics
Whose vibrations birth
Radiant possibilities

Come…come dance
Celebrating the new myth
You have etched within your heart

Festival of Light
Whose luminosity sets your sky
On FIRE

Come…come dance
In the Glory of your dreams
elegance draped in precious jewels of the Mystery playing as your form
Come…come dance…
For those who know GOD………………..Celebrate in the name of the Holy One

The tavern doors have been flung wide open
A rowdy crowd of mystics and whirling dervishes
Toast to your delight
Singing the hymn of your being and becoming
Outrageous verses they chant that
Glorify your intentions
Written from holy Light
Illuminating your pathway of tomorrow

The winds of the four corners
Carry your dreams forward

Seeding your tomorrows

today

Don't know what lies ahead

Yet FAITH sustains you

In the dramatic effects of light and shadow

Carving new landscapes with your mind

You can make anything happen

With the conviction of your FIRE

Intensity of your desire

Resuscitate your every dream

For nothing is too big in GOD

Nothing can deter your LIGHT

TRUTH amplified

Shouts your name from high above

That the angels rock in the heavens to your Holy YES

Celebrate….the GOOD that is yours

Reveling in your resplendent luminosity

Sing…the aria of your authenticity

Confidently moving in the direction of your dreams

Yes… this is the year of living outrageously

The never ending journey

Of the circular path of GOD

Creating in the streaming intensity of intention

Bring forth…in such courage…that which is within you

Elemental

Instrumental

No more black and white thinking

In the vastness of psychedelic possibilities

Imagine… your intentions a year from now

The deep sense of knowing

That all things are possible
Yes….all things are possible….in GOD….in LOVE

Take in this LIGHT….breathe in your GOOD….today….
you have taken the step confidently towards tomorrow
Dance…dance in the Beloved's delight who marvels at your
wonder. This is a moment to Celebrate!!!!

New Year Celebration 1.1.09

8. Surrender to the Darkness

Surrender

To the darkness

The fertile initiation

Provoked by the eclipse of the soul

Surrender

To the mystery

Of the pains of earth

The traverses of time

That linger

Penetrating and poignant

Breathing in to the density

Go within

To the recesses of your mind

Allowing the vestiges of the past

The lurking limitations

to reveal themselves

sit in the discomfort, the unease, the fear

the not knowing, any disappointment

Be in it....

Feeling...with every breath....feeling

In your human capacity

Human complexity

Knowing..

"the harder you resist, the harder it IS"

Deep into the "fruitful darkness"

The space from which

Compassion is called forth

Truth emerges from the crevices

Sit still

In the Silence as it

Takes you across this pass

Into the solitude of your soul

Die every moment

To the ego

Until little is left

Embrace the darkness

Pregnant potentiality, precious opportunity

Surrender

To the eternal center

Allowing...the penetrating shadows that surface

These prophets of transformation

to write a new gospel

Of the wounded healer

Who awakens

As you are rocked in the arms

Of the BELOVED

Into the "fruitful darkness"

a journey of time

into TRUTH

into LOVE

of SPIRIT

turning poison

into medicine

Drink of this deliberate infusion

Sit in the silence

Do not run or hide or lunge for the light

the secrets of the mystery

lie within the shadows

surrender to the formless one

enter deeper....deeper into the "fruitful darkness."

Good Friday, "The Fruitful Darkness" 4.10.09

9. Spirit Is Calling - Summer Solstice Celebration

Summer Dance

365 pirouettes
around a regal, luminous sphere
elegant Earth mother
meets fiery father sun
In a moment
Seemingly standing still
With the "arching Milky Way"
as their brilliant witness
Summer begins celestially
During this one long
solstice dance

However… movements of the season begin
prior to this calendar marking
officially .. summer kicks off
with school doors flung wide open
boys and girls race out
laughing, screaming
plotting joyful adventures
unbound hearts their perfect compass
ready to scoop up life's delicious offerings

Remember…. when we were kids

Days filled from head to toe
"breaking free of routine"
looking no further
than the present moment

so our imagination
could run free

sunrise lemonade sky
awakened us deep inside
enticed us out the door
for day long bike rides
playing basketball with the boys
cannon ball splashes at the neighborhood pool
collecting minnows from the pond
with your best friend
slip sliding and hula hooping like a fool
laughing at our
cherry slurpee brain freezes
melting with rainbow snocone delight
watermelon juice tye-dying our shirts
in luscious red
as peaches drenched us in their succulent love

Barefoot, bohemian days rolled by
lounging on peppermint striped blankets
beneath billowing, lingering clouds
moments measured not by time
but the length
of lurking shadows
hearts at peace
minds at ease
future selves
seeded in deep daydream visions
laying their innocently
listening to the laughter of stars
who shared the secrets
of their light.

SPIRIT called out boldly
Life answered with a HOLY YES
laughter of a child
filled each moment
with amazing GRACE

You see…

Summer is a feast
for senses and sensualness
Mother Earth teaches
her children
of such deliberate decadence
sun drunk Indian Paintbrushes
flirt with Mexican mad Hatters
White Rock Fields
who have gone daisy wild
spread gossip about illuminated matters
spring seeds meet their destiny
bearing fruits with such zesty flavors
tantalizing life
ignited by her inner fire
writes explicit love stories.

deep heated exhales of the season
sprinkle our salty, liquid pearls
upon the fields
one can hear the sigh of flowers
in utter relief
from the impersonal 100 degree heat

daily…change lingers on the edges of reality
spilling forth in dances
of light and shadows

summer transforms us deeply
just as caterpillars
move forward in their spring transformation
life unfolds
in single-mindedness
in radiant bliss of photons and form
the only rule existing
is to grow and play beyond the norm

Here we arrive
infused in this solstice light
the many revolutions
of our lives
bring us back to these simple desires
some of us have grown
confused by life's complexities
the innocence and presence of TRUTH
lost in the details of our adulthood
summer's expansive energy
invites us into awakened remembrance

Love calls us forth
SPIRIT's whispers
are answered by the seed
in the wisdom of her GLORY
a healing going on within
shapeshifts us
as we emerge into our greater story

As brighter days are summer's promise
holding light for those who do not see
something calling each of us
deeper —more than we seem to BE

TRUTH takes us higher
kissing the solstice sky
as the Sun
dances on earth's horizon
our soul is ignited
here on earth

SPIRIT is calling
inviting you to the wonder of your being
dance like a Sufi dervish
in the ecstasy of meaning
fall into the open fields
of infinite becomingness
as the promise of spring
led us out of the darkness
allow summer ignite you
in the HOLY YES

Be as little children
scooping up the day
in sweet innocence
allow yourself to PLAY
stay out until the sun sets
come home upon your soul's calling
remember life is for living
fulfilling SPIRIT's deepest longing.

Breathing in the Holy Now

Breathing in this Holy NOW
painted sky exhales
last light's
silent vow
marmalade promises of yet another day
sangria sunset kisses
never returning void
earth's Sufi dance around the sun
calls us in reflective prayer
time to come home
upon our mother's echoing refrain
back to where we belong
in the BELOVED's night embrace

Worn out but not weary
dusty but not down
overflowing cups
of sensualness
and dreams unbound.

SPIRIT called out so boldly
life sung its holy hymns
LOVE poured out through every pore
LIFE oozed from every whim
Summer grows us beyond our edges
LIGHT etches stories in INFINITE mind
our soul expands as exquisite glory
growing deeper and deeper
in appreciation of our time.

Breathing in this Holy NOW
day sanctified in awareness

Breathing in this HOLY NOW
life blessed with such Magnificence.

SPIRIT in me
quietly rests
SPIRIT in me
the mystery fully expressed

Summer Solstice Celebration   6.13.09

10. A Child's Wonder

In the stillness of winter

within the deep onyx silence

winds carry the story

of that one luminous night

An ancient promise

preceded TRUTH incarnate....

of LIGHT...

born of pristine awareness

wrapped in swaddling simplicity

the ornament of our remembrance.

Glorious heavenly hymns

punctuated by the star in the East

led Shepherds to the Christ child

adorned in awe and reverence.

Three magi followed the shining decree

bearing gifts of sweet, bitter fire and gold

a child laid there innocently

whose life would reveal

that we are WHOLE.

As the Christmas story unfolded

passed from generation to generation

songs emerged of our journey home to TRUTH

laced in every tradition.

Joy to the World and Holy Night

Santa's Baby and Chestnuts Roasting on an Open Fire

Prayers laid in verse and rhyme

activate the renewal of our hearts

Tis' the Season of remembering

of the gifts born of LOVE

In childlike wonder

vignettes of outer landscapes

are recreated within our homes

a remembrance of life's renewal

brought inside with evergreens and holly berries.

European villages with pubs and small churches

decorate our tables

strands of emerald, ruby, diamond colored brilliance

adorn the darkness around the Stable.

Every corner and crevice decorated in glitter glory

beauty transforming barren dreams

delicate ornaments reflecting our true story.

As the cold edge creeps upon us

in our daily routines

long gaps from the light

take us deep within.

Laying underneath the Christmas tree

gazing for hours like little children

the wonder of the Season fills us

in expansive awareness.

The fulfilled ancient promise

whose wisdom still speaks through the ages

calls forth an understanding

of our divine luminescence.

We twinkle like the stars

Joy electrifies the atmosphere

Contagious merriment seeps through every pore

as we gather to drink and dine

Traditions fill the plates with tamales, turkey, roast beast and rum balls eggnog lattes filled to the brim

there is plenty for ALL.

We take the time to circle up

travelling long distances like the magi

lavishing our bonds of love

letting the darkness know

there is only power in the LIGHT.

We celebrate those who have gone on before us

joyful expectancy of dreams that are being born.

We reminisce, laugh and sing Christmas Carols

as we look around in reverence and awe.

The Grinch can't steal it

the land of the Misfits mirror our perfect ways

Rudolph's shining nose leads us into authenticity

Frosty the Snowman ignites our inner JOY

Santa Claus comes bearing wrapped promises

which are actually exchanges of LOVE

Together we write new holy hymns

of our light that has come to earth

We gather to remember

the glory of our being

we gather to remember

the TRUTH of luminous seeing.

A child's wonder

was born

within each of us

in the story two thousand years ago

The seed of our Divinity

is celebrated with lovingly wrapped boxes and bows.

As the days move forward

Pause mindfully along the way

gaze into the stars of each other's eyes

Hug those who have touched you dearly

Remember friends who have brought

meaning and purpose to your life

Honor those who have tended to your dark night

With every connection stand in reverence

as we praise each other's Christ Child.

May you know that you are blessed.

May you know that you are light

With each Christmas Season

May you remember that you are LOVED.

CSL Mystic Note Holiday Celebration 12.5.09

11. Memory of the Future

In the dim awareness
skirting around the periphery
of ancestral memory
echoes of Divine remembrance reverberate
DNA encoded with light stir my soul.

A ghostlike embrace
of the Edenic experience lingers
like a love hangover.
There is a matrix tattoo
a blueprint of perfection
at the center of my being.

Faded vignettes of luminous living
cast shadows upon my mind.
I feel a restlessness
with illusion
As I open the portal of my heart
pulling me forward
gravity resists my intentions to soar
I fall backwards
pulled by density
slipping into amnesia
forgetting where I came from......Forgetting who I AM
<PAUSE>
In the stillness....
of the vast sapphire sky
I hear
A haunting voice
calling me....
Wake UP!

Wake UP!

Wake UP!

I hear her

in the Garden

laughing

questioning

I see the sideshow, talking snake

with all of his allure

dangling the fruit

...the fruit

that bears the secret

of that which has no beginning...no end.

I see her

taking it ..

the bite

of Divine Curiosity

a bold & courageous act

to taste time

to stand Naked to the Word

In **that** quantum shift

the morning star

came to earth

the I AM of eons

the I AM of the HOLY NOW

the I AM

emerged to look

into its own eyes

able to gaze at the Moon

It was a fall of Love into form

not a fall out of Grace.

Eve took a hike out of the Garden

A journey into self awareness

to see Original Wholeness
from the inside-out
she planted the seed deep within us
of the Lotus Flower of our being

Eve...the goddess of choice
passes me the palette of possibilities
I taste of the pair of opposites
savoring the succulence of life
dripping with mango, oozing bliss
then experiencing the crimson pain of a broken heart
One moment I am steeped
in joyful communion with
a rowdy crowd of mystics
the next, crushed by seeping sorrow
provoked by the violence all around me
Although I may not understand the paradox
I realize
sweet cannot exist without bitter
cold cannot exist without hot
a kiss cannot exist without the other
Thanks to Eve
I see you
I see me
Adam had someone to adore
The seeming separateness
is just a world of degrees
rainbow waves of light
playing interludes in between the veil.

In the slam poetry of life
elemental mandalas
rave on about the tales

of the descent of light into form
silence emerging as the Word
A saxophone, jazz kirtan
where East meets West
leads me to the deeper waters of stillness
In an intimate caress
the sun evaporates the misty memory
dramas disrobe in the nakedness of Reality
the mundane is resurrected in recognition
of Spiritual Truth seen without 3D glasses on
Eve left no footprints
like a cloud leaves no trail in the sky
Along the pathway of GOD
in the seeming forked road of duality
songs try to lure me back to the Garden
as I step forward on the Quest
Although cellular memory is deeply impaired
radiant remembrance
shimmers along the edges of my mind.
Yet…I look around
at the sleepwalkers
who never see beyond their past
transfixed, watching reruns
of the good ole days
Looking over their shoulder of how it once was
iphone maps synched to East of Eden
rearview mirrors of life their misguided compass
groupies still singing about Margaritaville
the Hail Mary touchdowns
linger like a trapeze artist who never lands.
Squatters in a house divided
Nostalgic entrapment of the Garden.

The Memory of the Future calls me
striving for the Greater Yet to BE
my soul leans into the Vision
the balance of one foot on earth
one foot in heaven
In the intimate communion
with light and shadows
I begin to see Paradise…
right here…right NOW
Purity of awareness
cleanse the muddied mind
GOD glimmers
reveal the spiritual as the material
Light unleashes her luminous hymns of creation
the secret of the Garden is discovered
as the kingdom of heaven within
the journey of awakening
takes me to a higher mountain view
co-creating my life in wonder and awe.

I'm reminded of the Master Teacher
the renegade, radical
who dissolved the gossamer veil of separation
ignited the world on fire
tossed out the money changers
pissed off the Pharisees
walked on water
then turned it into wine for the party
He never saw a cripple, drunk, thief or whore
he only saw their Wholeness.
He lived fearless of death
fiercely standing in ONENESS
The mountains shouted his name

the rocks answered his command
Lazuras got his dead ass up
the woman who touched his garment
began to Shine
He wasn't acting out, he was acting from
a Deep well of TRUTH
-------PAUSE---------
Let this calls us
"the Central Fire"
that transmutes all
"accumulated identities."
transcendent self emerges
Heaven as Earth
mystic mantra unleashes its POWER

The core of my being
Moves
the core of my being
awakens
the core of my being
dances
to my true identity

Sacred is it
this elixir of light
sacred is it
the seed of the Universe
as us
Sacred invitation
to awaken
One with the Muse
the Inner Presence
Divine essence

offering the fruit of Memory
of Original Wholeness

Taste with me this flower bearing gift
TRUTH
naked to the WORD
naked to LIGHT
naked to LOVE
into this pristine pool of awareness
dive with me into
into this holy verse
the very essence That You Are….
the I AM
I fall with you
In LOVE
I fall with you
In GRACE
I dance with you
In JOY…in Remembrance
together we stake our holy claim as you join me in unison …….. OM

"The Quest" Center for Spiritual Living, Dallas and Unity of Dallas May 5, 2010

12. Christmas At The Center

There's a charge in the air
With a cool, crisp kiss
The light is surrendering
As the Sun seems to be tucking himself to sleep

Fall is full of plates of bountiful harvest
Thanksgiving grace overflows
in crimson and amber celebrations

Something begins stirring
As soon as the last leftover is done
Suddenly we see Elves with green shoes on the Platform
Announcing their Santa's village is up and ready for FUN
Evergreens appear
having been mindfully selected
Ornaments of all shapes, colors and sizes
deck the halls in adornment
Petra who IS indeed a self-professed
Christmas nut
Has unleashed all of this magic
For tradition to be set up

With her red overalls on
with such utter delight
The goddess of Christmas
Calls forth the glow of first lights

Now Marsha, Now Alva, Now Chris and Dorayne,
On Melissa, On Veronica, On Dottie and Lainey
First Team ready with the 2011 Calendar already set

It's time to prepare
for Christmas at the Center

Hope counts tithes with a quiet Holiday hum
Sherry has the CORE Council wrapping gifts all night long
Alan is checking that AIS list twice
Santa knows we're New Thought
So there's no naughty or nice

The Stewardship team aligns all of the icicles on the windows
While the Vision Core downloads SPIRIT's perfect toy making instructions
The Nominating Core gathers you to lead Santa's Village
While the PR team has Mrs. Claus posting on Facebook

Practitioners have their stockings
Hung up in a row
Waiting for answered prayer
Knowing indeed that you are WHOLE
Chris has the Circles of Life
Lighting the way
Connecting you in Love
Every single day

Now we are an open minded community
We say come as you are
So you'll find some furry friends
like Snoopy, Winnie the Pooh and a Lorax
Sitting in the chairs….

Just watch out for the snake…
I'm not too sure about that one…
I think that it's actually Melissa's pet that got away
While she was working so diligently
on the Holiday Discover your Center

Christmas cheer is found everywhere you go
Jane answers phones with a hearty hello
Sally welcomes New Visitors with a twinkling smile
Virginia & Clyde take the Who's from Whoville on a lovely tour

There's a list of over 20 Greeters
Who welcome you with such glee
Ann, Sid, Donna, Carol, Eddie and Reagin
handing out hugs like peppermint candy

Raymond stuffs the Center's pamphlets
With a ho ho ho of joy and laughter
Angel Wings move mountains of letters of Gratitude

Joyce, once the leader of the animal ministry,
Now has a group knitting scarves for the non-furry
Veronica whose heart is two sizes too big
has the elves doing Community Service throughout the city.
Dorayne is upstairs with the Drummer Boy in YFM
Rudolph brought his Misfit friends who so Seamlessly fit- Perfectly in

Eggnog latte cups are recycled upstairs
Roast Beast is cooking in the kitchen by Marsha with such care
Hospitality Angels set up sugar cookies and snacks
Blessed by Dottie in all of her reverence

Christmas at the Center
Bringing Joy to the World
Dawn has draped every crevice and counter
In emerald, silver and golden bows
Susan's Wonderful Life train chug-chugs along in the foyer
Ruth is tiding up waiting for the three Magi.

Richard is up through the night
to catch the Grinch on film
Realizing it's Joe Tinker stealing Christmas cookies
with that wicked grin.
Jason and the A/V team beaming lights like Rudolph
As the musicians in their holiday sway
Jam with Gary and Julie knocking the roof off.

Dashing on the stage
Stars dancing in the night
The Music team with
the Celestial Choir
are singing like angels on high
Alva is Knowing All Things are Possible in GOD
While there are Christmas Carols led by Lainey
a Jewish girl who is New Thought

Rebecca guides the silence of the deep Taize
Connecting in our hearts
With the Great Master Teacher
Into the Silent Night
We fall with Grace and Ease
Knowing his "law is love
His gospel is peace"

Here at the Center
We don't write lists or think about wishes
We affirm and declare
Celebrating all of our demonstrations
Yes….we wrap them in Magnificence
Sprinkle them with glitter
All the while we know
The Perfection of SPIRIT

There are too many names to name
In such a simple poem
Each one of you is what makes this community so strong
I have etched your Love on
multi-colored strings of light
adorning this Sanctuary
on this Holy Night

Underneath the Mistletoe
Waiting for that Divine Kiss
Nestled by the fire of Love
The Presence as our GIFT
Wrapped up in Beauty, Wonder and Awe
This IS the GLORY of who we really ARE

I can hear the GOOD Rev. Dr. proclaim
on the Mountaintop of Truth
Your Luminous Name

Christmas at the Center
Together in LOVE
A Home for the Holidays
A place for our Hearts.
Merry Christmas!!

Center for Spiritual Living, Dallas   Mystic Note All-Star Holiday Show   December 4, 2010

13. Love, Beatles Styles

Love, love me do
A love that was so lyrical and true
With Beatlemania
an electric light pulsating
swirled all around the world in a frenzy
with every girl screaming
What was happening
wasn't just a wild, cultural revolution
It was millions of hearts ....exploding
Being broken.... wide open

In this cosmic, ecstatic romance
Love, Beatles style arrived in a euphoric measure
They ignited the Infinite Power of that four letter ELIXIR
whose perfect touch imprinted upon me melodies
Making me feel happy deep inside
With promises to be true... sending me all of their loving day & night
Awakening that ultimate longing.

They taught me the path of devotion
To give and receive such adoration
As I stumbled along the growing edge of innocence
blossoming into romance
I longed to understand
This connection of the heart
A love beyond logical whose taste was so mystical
Then it happened....I saw her standing there... way beyond compare
A fire washed over me consuming my senses
With that magnetic compulsion I had to be in her presence
Wanting to hold her hand
Someone to love, someone to please

With the Fab 4 tunes humming beneath my being
I knew she'd love me like no other <<She Loves You – Music>>

As the earth wouldn't dance with another
In it's slow tango around the sun
with every revolution in my journey
I surrendered to the possibility of two souls merging
Within the arms of belonging
Enamored in those rhythmic gospels
I tye dyed the night like the aurora borealis
shouting "I love you, I love you" - 8 days a week

One day ….I awoke in such pure awareness
dissipating that dualistic haze
I heard a voice say
Listen…..do you want to know a secret
Come closer and I will reveal it….
As I stood still in the temple of my being
suddenly flooded with LIGHT
I realized each time my heart melted for another
…..……I was falling in love with GOD

Thus began my dance with the Divine
All I could see from then on were
Radiating faces of Magnificence
Whose lips I longed to kiss..whose essence I wanted to embrace
I began to understand the deeper mystery
Of living with a heart wide open

The secret I wanted to know
Became clear to me
Was this thing called Life
The one I was seeking
Is the lotus of my heart

What is breathing as me through me
Is a LOVE not known by words or touch
Whose origin is the very hymn of my being
Whose Purity… Deconstructs every story
A love that I can't hide
A love so deep inside

Breathe in with me..
A fire so pure
Imagine a world of Peace ignited by unconditional LOVE
Heaven right here on Earth.
So close your eyes
And I will kiss you
with all my heart
I send to you…..
These promises of TRUTH
With every heartbeat
I unleash this secret
Of this ecstatic romance
The Beloved who drums
The very essence that is our DANCE…
I offer this…..as a blessing..
With all my loving.

Winter Solstice Celebration, Dallas, TX – "Imagine Peace"   *December 17, 2010*

14. Look In The Mirror

Look in the mirror
Tell me….
What do you SEE?

Do you see the brilliance of your being
Luminous windows of your inner sky
cascading as the peppermint pink dawn
awakening you into magnificence?

Do you believe in
The power of who you are
Pure awareness wrapped in turquoise silk shawls of possibilities
Inspired by your genius?

Can you catch your own smile
that is a contagious beam
healing strangers who glimpse it
emanating compassion that becomes a tidal wave of GOOD?
Can you bear witness
to the intensity of your greatness
Like the Milky Way laying down tracks of LIGHT
Impressing upon the universe Wonder & Awe

OR…. are you bound by ancient stories
denigrating tales, some more subtle than others
that deny the Glory of Life
Believing you are only dust
From which you shall return
Yet your essence is not of some lowly nature
It is the rainbow light particles that are slow dancing as your form
Pulsating as your being

It takes great courage to awaken from deep slumber
To break free like the seed in the fruitful darkness
That hears the hymns of its own greater story
Being called forth
Into Beauty Realized

It takes mindfulness
To contemplate your inner heaven
while standing in the midst of a storm
Your roots strong, every fiber of your being grounded in
Peace

It takes great humility
to heal the sins of the father
Instantly…with LOVE
unveiling your glorious nature encoded as DNA
the Mystery made manifest as YOU

Look in the mirror
To understand your significance in this world
For a constellation is not made of just one star
Your uniqueness added to the palette of earth
Paints hues of luscious landscapes

Look in the mirror…..
Praising your gifts
In this elemental, ecstatic dance
Dissipating stories that have dragged doubt along your path for too long
Groove in freedom to unleash your LIGHT
Remaining fluid as Grace flows as the River of YES

We are here to sing our soul's song of Peace
To be that we wish to see
Disarming the weapons of thought, words & deeds

being called into great Mastery
of service to a larger Vision
igniting our dreams into being.

So…look in the mirror….
See what I SEE……be dazzled by it all…the GLORY of your ESSENCE.

The Sound of Peace Concert   *1.28.11*

15. We Are Called

We are called
To be fully orbed and alive
to awaken to the intricate
Details the Divine lays out before us
Balinese floral offerings
Every single day
To the GOD within

Early morning raspberry love notes etched upon the cobalt sky
With Venus winking
Reminds me to drink this concoction of Love & Light daily
So it will beam from my eyes
Emanate from my being
the celestial mirror to live from a colorful, bold perspective
paints my world out of a palette of beauty and not brokenness

The intricate masters of nature remind me
There is no tempest destroying our power
or a tempter leading us astray
There is only LOVE
Deep within us
Bring us to the awareness of the Everyday Sacred

Spirit is always calling
Awakening deep within
The Mystery that adorns the world with our gifts
Spirit is calling
To place offerings of unconditional love
to everyone we meet
through our song and our smiles
the elixir of our true nature

We are GOD
Star seeds within us
Stirring
The elemental fusion
Birthing a new way of being
Complacency
Is Divine Discontent

Spirit is calling
It is time unleash your light into the world
We must be like the seed
In the "fruitful darkness"
Compelled to push upward
Or around granite obstacles
Seeing that one sliver of yes
Like a Houdini move
the impulsion of LIFE
To express
Is beyond any resistance
More powerful than any NO

We are not here for a theological debate
Or the resurgence of myth
Deep is calling upon deep
Spirit is calling
For heaven as earth
As the flower reminds us
Of the universe contained within
We are being called
As the GLORY of GOD
To exude WONDER & AWE
To live from the fullness and wholeness
Of our being
To answer only to the Master within

Not a story deficient of meaning
SPIRIT is calling
for this conscious dance
for this ecstatic, Divine romance
to fall in love 10 million times
in a day
setting the world on FIRE
with JOY

2.26.11

16. A Seed Within

A seed deep within the "fruitful darkness"
is stirred by an inner Light
Encoded within it indigenous nature
is an Original Blessing
that compels itself to awaken
moving through layers of the mystery
breathing in as it breaks out of its small story
persistent in it's unfoldment towards the unknown
finally, resolutely, blooms as its magnificence.
No granite boulder or paved sidewalk
or even a desert drought of excuses
Can contain its Glory
In that moment of individual awakening
It finds itself living
In radical interdependence in the heart of GOD as all existence
In this elemental dance called Life

The seed mirrors your journey
The Mystery encoded as your being
Seeking to bloom boldly like the irises singing holy hymns of lavender
Your soul's charge is to live out loud in fuchsia hallelujahs of a sunrise
To raise the roof of consciousness
Reflecting the cosmos here as Earth
Even in the subtle pretenses of duality
The Light is present as YOU etching poetry out of every moment.

Ten thousand white lotus petals
Exist as your heart
Luminous is your nature
Dancing in 3D adventures
Your soul seed of Radiant mind awakens

To the Flame and the Light
That You Are
An intuitive compass
Your GPS - God positioning system
Guides you home

In this sanctuary you entered
the Divine greets the Divine
with an open heart, a deep Recognition
Here...in this common Unity of Diversity
Ignited by the fire of **transformation**
Your Genius is unleashed into the Infinite Playing field
That is the Delight of the DIVINE
Together, as we taste Freedom like we've never known
We write new parables of conscious evolution
Discovering Wholeness in emerald revelations
bringing you to this new declaration
Celebrating connections through laughter, joy and bittersweet tears

In this sacred mandala of community
In the adoration and appreciation of your luminosity
We receive you unconditionally & authentically
The Gifts you bring are precious & powerful
Through inspiration and imagination ...... Expansive and expressive
With the potency of prayer............... Grateful that we are together
we create new sets of wings woven in Truth
to launch our every dream and desire.
This safe place to land becomes the portal of possibilities
Grounded in principle, pulled by a vision, led by LOVE.

There are those who have come before us
There are those here to guide you along the way
Supporting your Magnificence
Through soul's on FIRE and meaning making moments

Sacred celebrations, rituals and potlucks

We write a new myth of GOD

In this elemental dance of self-discovery of your WHOLENESS

the seed that is your LIGHT reveals exquisite Perfection

We build a new earth, through every intention.

We create a world free to live by the highest expression.

Yes…You are Home… in this sacred space that you Belong.

Yes…you are supported in more ways than you will ever know.

Yes…we are here to walk with you as you SHINE ON!

"A Seed Within" New Member Sunday – Center for Spiritual Living, Dallas   *11.20.11*

17. Most Wonderful Time of the Year

The leaves have completed their fall pirouettes
Pumpkin pie colors lavish the land punctuated by gold
The electrifying chill in the air heralds the season we approach
Yes…it's the most wonderful time of the year

A magical stirring mysteriously releases
Invisible Elves throughout our neighborhoods
Dark streets at night are transformed into rainbow displays
While Frosty, Santa and the Three Shepherds share prime front yard space

I listen to Michael Buble belt out Christmas tunes like Bing Crosby
I'm dancing in my car to Jingle Bell Rock
I go about my day humming every Christmas Carol I know
Singing pa rump pa pa pum and anything about snow

Sleigh Bells ring in my mind as I drive
I hear Santa calling Rudolph and the Reindeers on 635
Sentimental feelings roll through shopping at Whole Foods
I look for mistletoe everywhere to give more kisses to my Beloved

The hustle and bustle of the season kicks off with eggnog lattes & extra espresso
But it's the family Tamale making weekend that means the most
Thousands of Sugar cookies overflow from kitchens in town
The city lights up with smiles and the warm hellos all around

We send our greetings on Facebook and Twitter
We Skype to our loved ones living in other cities
But there is nothing more sacred than sitting with each other
Keeping our promise of being home for the holidays.

The contagious laughter of children fills the atmosphere with glee

Their innocence reminds us what it's like to be free

Their certainty of Santa Claus causes me to reflect

To focus on my GOOD and not the things I regret.

Evergreens wrapped in Silver and sapphire ribbons

With angels on high bring us to our knees in such reverence

The lights on the trees trigger something within

They are the souls of our ancestors winking at us.

The Holy Child that inspired this night

With the ancient ritual of the darkness greeting the Light

Weave together in such a mystical way

That we let go of our stories of separation on this Day

Songs carried by the wind of the festivities of the Season

Bring us out of our doubt and fear, into receiving

For it's not the ribbons, bows and the presents we give

It is the LOVE that we share, the LIFE that we LIVE

It's as if we enter a timeless dimension

Suddenly we are filled with treasure of our ONENESS

In such profound JOY & perfect remembrance

We celebrate the faithful friends & family who are dear to us.

Here is what an angel once shared with me –

Taking nothing for granted

Make each moment precious

Spend time with your loved ones

Present to their essence

Pause and contemplate the story of the star

For it is the true Light of who we are

As the days go by, the seasons roll through

We are reminded at Christmas
Of the Christ that is in me and you…
Go out & glow in this holiday cheer
Staying in the BLISS…making it the most wonderful time of the year.

Mystic Note Holiday Show CSL Dallas   *December 3, 2011*

18. I Made A Promise

I made a promise
Before I surfed to earth
That I would
Only remember LOVE
Signing on the luminous line
That my heart would remain wide open
No matter what
Peeking prematurely behind the emerald velvet curtain
Seeing God
Only the DIVINE
With all of these clever characters with their quirks and personalities
Dressed in interesting, intricate costumes with outrageous rituals of separation
I placed my ticket on heaven's counter
Shouting whoohoooo
I'm IN

The day I was born
I hung a Post It Note
On Infinity
A constellation that was my code
Of remembering
To be awake
At this time
As we move through wormholes
And discover our galactic center
Shaking off old paradigms
Rising to a higher way of living

I chose to come here
I agreed to play in this game
Wearing blindfolds for a while

Even with the connections I had with the stars

Those quantum clues I saw

in the innocence of my childhood

whispered to me that I was here for the LIGHT

Always and only for LOVE

No matter what the world said

Yet…Along the way I got distracted

Somehow I ate the apple

Probably in a fried pie

Fell asleep like Snow White

Forgetting my true Life

Tripped down some rabbit hole

Like Alice

With distorted views

Wearing those dualistic, 3D lens

I was a bit confused

Landing on my face

Naively believing in Grace

In between tequila shots and Corona with 2 limes

Lost in my 20s in the dance of false celebration….I was desperately seeking GOD

In all of the wrong places

I believed in LOVE and only LOVE

Yet my vulnerable heart took me down dark roads

Time and time again broken promises

Constructed a gigantic iron wall of distrust

Keeping me dense

Keeping me in defense

Even though I had dreams

I was keeping them

Locked in the dungeon

Guarded by imaginary dragons

It was either my voice

Or God's voice

Or the angels

Inside my head

That kept me moving in the right direction

Spirit calling me

Lifting me up

Dusting me off

Shifting mountains that were really mole hills

In between the others who snuck in

Those shifty shadows

Like subtle bullies

Belittling me into submission of less than

Whether it was being in the presence

Of someone who acted as if I was invisible

Collecting do not pass Go cards

In the game of life

When all I got were no's slammed in my face time after time

Heart shattered into a million shards

That I threw up into the sky to become stars

a powerful force kept me alive

Faith in a greater GOOD pulsed through my being

A faint mist of a greater possibility at the periphery of my mind

Pulled me towards my vision time and time again

Doors opened left and right

Adventures were lining up all through my life

I actually had more joy than distress

But I was still stuck feeling a heavy chain around my neck

I had friends who adored me

I worked in a city of heightened ego arrogance

I couldn't watch the news without regret

There was still some intense
Divine Discontent

Many nights I spent Wondering driving along the PCH
With the window rolled down
Ocean waves in their jazz melodic groove
The stars lining the horizon as I drove north
The salty scent saturating my senses keeping me present in my body
Thinking I don't belong on this planet
What kind of crazy world would be so f-ed up
So painful
Why would people have forgotten their original essence
Destroying each other with such vengeance
Living at the lowest common denominator
mental terrains That I refused to traverse
I would cry, cry, cry.. a deep sorrow
Pleading to be taken home
Back to the stars where I belong

I lived for the Light, never laying claim to the darkness
Spending time cleaning up the clutter of condition
Standing firm in the Power of the Presence
something was always there
Stirring like the seed at the end of winter
With an appointment to bloom in spring
Something that would not abide
By the contradictions

Unsettled........Unsatisfied
I rocked back and forth from heaven and earth
In contempt of duality
Needing to make peace with this present reality
I would go to the mountains
Hang out with the Sequoias

Chant with the rivers

talking to the heavens all night long

Spirit was calling me

To remember that Post It Note

The promise I made to myself

To know that it is all GOD

Spirit calling

Deeply

An impulse of fire within me

Igniting the fusion of this elemental dance

Stirring, stirring me into shaking off the stories

Collapsing the stale vignettes to unleash my GLORY

It took a catastrophe of immeasurable pain

Which is actually not necessary

Illness leading me through the inner labyrinth

To find my Holy name

In the presence of my pint sized gurus

Rising like the Phoenix

Finding a conscious community

That was all about transformation

I transmuted poison into medicine

I found my way home

I unlocked the code to the kingdom within

I awakened to the Wholeness of my being seen and unseen

Unleashing my light

Through the power of my word

The luminosity of my life

Spirit is calling

Always calling

Deep unto deep

It is relentless in reminding me

Of the beauty of my being
Although this is the ride I signed up for
The riddle I promised to break
I am here to tell you
We no longer have time
To stay asleep
The PRESENCE is being called forth
For each one of us to be AWAKE
Consciousness is paving the way
For a brand new earth

Now is the time
Here is the space
Spirit is calling each one of us
To unleash our GIFTS......

19. It's My Story and I'm Not Sticking To It

It's my story....

and I'm not sticking to it

I told a friend tonight.

A simple phrase

of letting go

triggered a contemplative shower

that not only lathered me in lavender

sweet scents for my body

but bathed me in the softness

of remembering my past

without the harshness of judgment

or deadweight of guilt.

Funny stories mixed with

mendacious musings

of a monkey mind

gone wild.

Old tales of shadow dances

Wanderings of a lost soul

in my early years

whose twists and turns

of many miles traversed

finally led to the gates

of Paradise found behind the superficial wall

of conditions.

A long journey

it seemed

of a life led by illusion

and confusion.

Recounting tales along the way

of being SPIRIT in form

human emotions mixed with chaotic energies

an interesting blend

of latte filled with LIGHT and DARK

infusions of my humanity.

Doubt, fear, neglect of my sweet self

That led to self destructive tendencies

as deterrents of my TRUTH.

I was blessed though

Angels along the way

nudged me as they knew

so absolutely knew

the TRUTH of my BEING

and saved me from drowning from my

wretched drunkenness of deceit.

One candle flame, one flicker of LIGHT

is all that is needed to dispel the darkness

One unconditional "I love you"

Spoken as a proxy

until I could hear the ONE

through my intuition and meditation

until whispered through my lips

of the inner recognition of my MAGNIFICENCE

until I tasted the ONE

and lit the FIRE within.

A silent glance, a gentle kiss, a firm hug

a tough stance, a steadfast best friend, a forever embrace

from someone who saw beyond the earth games

playing out in the theatrics of my life

kept me alive

all those years.

Saints in drag

dancing as lovers, friends and strangers

kept me from imploding.

A journey of a thousand nights

and ten thousand tears

that fed the fertile soil of fear and forgetting

which later became compost

for fields of golden GRACE and GRATITUDE

as I now savor the nectar of my ESSENCE

through the sweetness of the ONE

as my soul _expression.

Shadow dancers

took me through the crevices of fragmented light

my life purpose buried deep

beneath the layers of a wounded ego

squeezed in between the corners of a stained mind

from the race consciousness leaking through

and familial patterns

that haunt like hungry ghosts

generation after generation

genetic guises

recycled patterns

cluttering my life

the subterranean rivers of poisoned thoughts

that kept me from seeing my GOOD

from being my TRUTH

from dancing in my LIGHT.

That was part of my story

in between the joys and loves

of a life that touched other lives

which even then

old cards that testified to my soul strokes

and unconditional support

that I generously shared

weren't enough to remind me

at times of the love I really had

and the LOVE I really AM.

When I only saw the speck in the window

instead of the panoramic vista

of life's exquisite BEAUTY

all around and within.

Reruns are no longer welcomed

Toxic drips of tainted minds

cannot seep through.

A polished mirror

reflecting the most intimate secret of LIFE

that indeed I AM ONE

expressing so uniquely as me through

guides my days and nights.

As all of the bit players of my life

and melodramatic menaces

were the masters of their own drama

weaving intricate textures of duality

into my story

These are the moments of being human

that I cherish

when I can reflect on the chapters of my life

see the scenes that claim a space

in the unfolding of my life's mystery theater

while merely being

energy in motion

SPIRIT seeking to express itself

even in the midst of my ego

creating the illusion

of permanence

when in fact

effect is not my SOURCE.

I have never stopped expanding

only ignored the obvious

beneath the glaring LIGHT

that is ME shining through.

I still simmer in disappointment and droplets of confusion

I deal with drive by divas and almost lovers

as well as half ass friends

who highlight the dualistic tendencies

of the lower ego

even as I slightly judge them

until I see beyond the condition

that masquerades as pain and power

and the twinges of my psyche

stroking my ego.

I AM now awakened with affirmations

and LOVE infusions

and when I forget

ever so slightly

as I edge towards reversing

ever so briefly

I can count on

the ones who adore me

to bring me gently back

to the TRUTH

of the LOVE that is GOD

of the JOY that is SPIRIT

of the LIGHT that is LIFE

of the GOOD that is MINE.

I have many stories.

I'm not sticking to any of them.

Although there are some that I do cherish

the ones when I float in LOVE

and dive into ECSTACSY

of a first kiss

or a tangerine sky

a favorite friend

or the sweetness of a baby's breath.

I thank them, ALL of them, for the revelations and releases

that have brought me to the PRESENCE

in this very present moment that is my LIFE.

For this is what makes me human

while being SPIRIT

but is not the TRUTH of my ESSENCE

just the entertainment of _expression

as me through me.

7.22.06 12:36 am

20. Spirit Is Calling 2

Music cannot compel you
When your hands cover your
Ears

Poetry won't stir you
When your heart has been closed for so many
Years

A Mango Tango sunset won't be able to
Heal your blindness with your eyes
Shut.

A fire of Love
Won't keep you warm at night when you stand outside
Alone

Yet like the seed
Something begins stirring at the remembrance of
Light

Spirit is calling you awake
In the awareness of the Mystery that is your
Life

Gifts ready to adorn the world
Like the constellations of a beautiful summer
Night

Primordial ecstasy bursts forth
the elemental dance of a new
Star

Your name is your nature
An elixir of TRUTH in this world of
Form

Spirit is calling you deeply
To paint the world in Wonder and
Awe

Answer boldy the call sharing your LOVEsong in this world
Dazzle me with brilliance for you are the Divine on Earth.

2.26.11

21. What is it?

What is it....that has been following you like a shadow dancer
Discursive thoughts that trip you into duality
Head first

What is it .... Each thing you have been carrying around
Like a worn out, disheveled coat of dreams
Stained in disappointments, worries crumpled in inner pockets

What is it...that you hear....
echoes of a shattered heart
broken into a million shards of excuses whose edges come dangerously close
to cutting your Light from sight

These burdens that you carry....what are they....whose are they...
Dense.....Intense...Chewy....coalesced thoughts of self inflicted judgment
Lingering visions that haunt like hungry ghosts
whose veneer of joy covers the pain, the pressure of waiting, the unforgiveness

What are these old platitudes
Playing in your mind like an archaic jukebox
Whose songs of regret
Impose restrictions on your creativity
Memories that have captivated your attention sideways for too long
needing to be released and let go....

What are these broken promises that you keep wedged in between the doorway
Of your intentions and demonstrations
Trying to shut your heart from wide open wonder
Whose LOVE is so potent it would incinerate your every denial

What is this Doubt trying to suppress every single YES
that is reaching its way up to the sky to unleash your GLORIOUS NATURE
and illuminate the world in your Beauty & Power

Breathe …. Deeply …. Into this awareness….of those sublime projections
Of the myth of separation
That has tried to denigrate your Magnificence

Breathe..Deeply….into this awareness
Of the journey of being Spirit in human form
as your path criss-crosses the paradox of light & shadows
Weaving tapestries of your LIFE that is the Mystery made manifest

Lay down your burden
Give up that false foundation of confusion
It doesn't serve you
In this beautiful house of the Beloved that is your LIFE

Lay down your burden
Releasing those incessant refrains of innuendos of less than
Give them up
throw them into the fire
Like raku transmuting them into elegant art for your pleasure

Release….all of those moments that you have frozen in time in your mind
The should have, could have, would haves that linger like squatters
the vapid voices of shame & blame that are whispers of darkness

Breathe….deeply…. into this awareness…..of the misnomers
who laid claim to your holy essence…

Release them.....simply release your burdens….those thoughts that are
not your TRUTH…those situations that are chants of the past

Stand before them…eye to eye….calling their bluff..seeing

beyond their disguise..Discovering your Wholeness

Like the mist evaporating as the sun sensually caresses it with morning, golden kisses

Illuminate those places that call for forgiveness & healing

Igniting transformation….to reveal your GOOD

Be Free…yes.. FREE….to Celebrate Connection to SPIRIT …So

disintegrate those stories…drop those burdens you've been carrying …for they

hold no power over you in this Holy NOW.…

With a simple gaze..like a yogic, eagle pose….look clearly at these

dark gifts that are now calling forth your LIGHT

With pristine awareness …. Release them……Release them into the Fire..of ONENESS

Center for Spiritual Living, Burning Bowl Ritual   *1.1.11*

22. Original Essence

You are Pristine Light
Housed in an opulent temple
Dwelling in the matrix of Divine experiences

The secret of GOD
is the radiant text
written as You.
Sacred is your Original Essence
Encoded in your DNA
Is the Holy Sutra
of cosmic JOY
the Beloved's promise spoken and unspoken
that pulsates as your very heart beat.

Elegant waves of LOVE
Sculpt your WONDER and BEAUTY into being
Tending to the Blue-White ray of your LIGHT
In this spin of the Wheel of Life
GOD dropped into this dimensional grid
Through a portal of love
Ignited by a passionate kiss.
The soul seeking a place to express
In this quantum playground
Came forth AS YOU.

Call of the ancestors
is the hymn of remembrance
of the timeless
that slow dances as time
Born yet unborn
Form yet not contained by form

Seen yet unseen
Full in the emptiness
Power in the deep stillness
The Mystery that
Robes itself in golden saris, turquoise tunics
Even in blue jeans & cowboy boots

The ancestors slow fusion of rhythm & blues
Play as backdrop music
In these wave particle movements
We call Community Theater
That is the GOOD of LIFE of GOD expressing
Duality dipped in sensuality
Stirs into remembering
the original blessing
that is your exquisite nature.
The sacredness of who YOU are.....
Heaven AS earth

So PERFECT are you
That the pink flamingo sunset writes love notes to the Milky Way with your LIGHT

So PRECIOUS are you
That the Aurora Borealis drapes you in emerald veils like royalty

So DELICIOUS are you
That the rivers rush to merge with your ocean bliss & drink of your fountain of TRUTH

This Soulfest is about YOU
A celebration of Light.......Of Life

Reach in and rejoice
Let go of the archaic jukebox
Of broken stories

Give up wrestling with the angel of doubt and fear

Clean your shoes off the mess of conditioning

Turn up your LIGHT

Turn on your LOVE

And blind me with your brilliance

Unleash your Genius

with this palette

of kaleidoscope possibilities

Of vibrant hues that is your SPIRIT

Painting the world as your sweet humanity

IGNITE your Divinity

Setting this world on FIRE

in unconditional LOVE

beginning within YOU

Let's move to the groove

of the ONE

as the MANY

Together

we remember

we are WHOLE

and HOLY

Unbound

Set FREE

To raise the roof

Off this cosmic temple

Singing the lovesongs

Of our Original Essence

Living from our space

Of true GREATNESS

Performed at "Soulfest"---Unity Grapevine   6.26.10

23. Come Closer

Come closer
So you can see what I see
Exquisite hues
Of saffron, marmalade, fuchsia hellos
Of God

Come closer
So you can be what is yours to Be
Great Glory
Of Love, Abundance, Wisdom, Harmony
And more

Come closer
Dive into this sea of secrets
Jellyfish who light up within
To remind you of the luminosity
Of Life

You have spent eons blind
To the voice of the unknown
Mystery disguised as fear
Tripping you up into drinking bad beer
Of amnesia

It is time to awaken to the Truth
You are the ONE hidden in the wildflower fields
Screeching like the Milky Way
Of your immense glow of being
Seeing your ultimate reality
That is LOVE

Go on with yourself
Get back into the groove
Of living out loud
From the deepest caverns
Of understanding
That all of this is GOD.

5.15.14   10:30am

24. I Step Into the Darkness

I step into the darkness

Take me now.
Take my sorrows.
Take my tears
Take my fears

Weave a new blanket
Made of the stars.

I step into the darkness

To be free
From the shadows
Who haunt me
Like hungry ghosts
Lounging in the living room
Of my mind
Etched as fog
The amnesia of the fall
That really was an awakening

I step into the darkness
Only so I can see the light
Only so I can see in between
The lines of laughter and heartbreak
Only so I can mend what has never been broken
My heart
Whose light moves and grooves
As the rhythmic hymns of my being
Living, loving, grieving and regretting
A tapestry of my journey.

I step into God

Because it knows no pair of opposites
It dances with itself
Infinitely, over and over
Mirrors the possibilities
Of falling into Grace
In between the torn skirts of the veil
That simply is a game
To wake me up to Love
Whose key is deep inside.

5.15.14 10:09 am

25. I stood on the grass

I stood on the grass
The dew cleansing me
From any residual dreams
The dark clouds moved
Swiftly across the sky
In their mindfulness walkabout
The moon gazed upon me
With her gentle blessing
Of seeing my Light
An unknown friend
Winked at me
From millions of miles in the sky

I awakened in the early hours
To rise up to the Love
Of the One as me

Letting Go
Letting GOD
A little word for the Infinite Mystery
I breathe in Gratitude
I exhale Light
In the Grace of another day
I etch my morning
With Love notes of Life
A reminder for us to Play.

5.22.14   6:18 am

26. Who are you talking to?

Who are you talking to?

With all of that language

Of separation

Doubt

Limitation

constraints of the mind

The butterflies will not put with it

The redwood trees will contest it

The mockingbird will not sing it

For they know

About your secret

Yes...

The secret of your Light

The majesty of your essence

The exquisite dance of creation

That is your elevation

Of awareness

Of looking into the mirror

And seeing only GOD.

Who are you talking to?

That's right....

The ONE within.

No more nonsense, please

We've had enough of your harsh wind

Blowing dust in other's eyes.

Get up off your mat, Lazarus

Dance in the Light of the ONE.

27. Daily Hellos – 2007

One white flower
Held the secret of the universe
The Buddha knew
Mahakashyapa smiled
Do you see
the TRUTH?
So simple.

LOVE creates the world.
JOY and LAUGHTER
sustain it
Create
Dance
Twirl on the axis of TRUTH

What if I am just a dot
in someone's painting
red upon yellow
green upon orange
mixture of LIGHT and SHADOW
to create a whole
illusion.
Interesting.

Evolution
Is a spiraling
of your thoughts
higher and higher
into CREATIVITY

Raindrops
are ocean waves
travelling great distances
to tickle you
one wet kiss
at a time

I saw GOD today
She looked
Just like...
YOU!

My mind is telling me
Not to think so much
Just BE
PRESENT
to the PRESENCE
in between the tango
of thoughts.
Shhhhhhhhhh. Listen.

Wrap your MIND
around TRUTH
Watch your dreams
unfold PERFECTLY

Conscious choices
Create
a BEAUTIFUL world
Paint from your HEART

The Universe is here
to support you
how do you wish to PLAY??

A great DIVINE LOVE
Flows as YOU
through YOU
Dance ON in DELIGHT!!!

Evolution
means leaving behind
the baggage of the past
Are you ready
to clean
the closet of
your cluttered mind................BE FREE!

JOYFUL EXPECTANCY
Celebrate the GOOD
that is your
DIVINE INHERITENCE

SPEAK SIMPLE
for TRUTH
is ELEGANT

A clouded mind
Makes for a messy
manifestation
Clean up your
thoughts
with TRUTH.

Open new doors
By choosing new thoughts
The path is always
illuminated
by LOVE.

Release the games
of those dang monkeys
stop chasing
the circus in your mind
Recognize SPIRIT
Realize the DIVINE
in every moment
Let the monkeys
play somewhere else.
CLARITY.

DIVINE patterns
Tapestry of LIFE
What are you weaving
with your
words?
Flimsy blanket of excuses
Or silk shawls
of DELIGHT

A radiant smile
melts the walls of indifference
Recognizing GOD
in each other.
SMILE

TRUTH in a droplet
LIGHT in a kiss
LOVE in a smile
JOY in a HUG
GOD dancing
as me.........as you
as LIFE.

Naked
Is our Mind
Naked to LOVE
Naked to TRUTH
Naked to JOY
For separation
thinly veiled cloaks of condition
cannot keep you apart
from the ONE

Is it really true
when someone else's story
is smothered in fear
and uncertainty?
No.
So why even give it thought
droplets of confusion
dilute your intuition
cleanse it
with TRUTH
which is
GOD speaking

Winds whip the trees
into shape
Strengthening their roots
Pushing and pressing
them into being
with invisible power
RESLIENCE
Remember this
when life
whips you around
for you are building

a strong foundation
grounded in your TRUTH
knowing that indeed
it is
ALL GOD
ALL GOOD.

One thought
creates your reality
Look around
What's been on your mind
lately.
Hmmmm.

In the moment of
Recognition
I postmark Infinity
with a stamp of
I AM GRATEFUL
for the experience
that brought me
to the PRESENCE
in the present
the dance
of LIGHT and SHADOWS
Heaven as Earth

GRATITUDE
is finding GOD
in the details
of LIFE
kissing it
hello
in every moment

Mala bead bracelets
of blessings
that I wear around my soul
Mantras of
Remembrances
of the GOOD
received
GRACE given
GIFTS of SPIRIT
in the preciousness
of LIFE.
GRATITUDE
is a gift
for my sweet soul

Take a moment
to BREATHE
in the sacredness
of being
SPIRIT
as YOU.
Ahhhhhhhh.

In the beginning
was LOVE
She danced
as LIGHT and JOY
and became
YOU

Disappointment
is a measuring stick
swung around by my ego

Expectation

is a ruler

that sets limits

to what I desire

How about just being

PRESENT to the PRESENCE

as IS.

So much easier

When you slip into amnesia

Heart to heart resuscitation

is the only way

to awaken

from the illusion

Remember

GOD IS INDEED ONLY LOVE.

5.15. 14   10:23am

28. Blue Door Cusco

Peruvian pathways
Granite blocks of moved mountain
Winds of time have shaped you
Hands of man have placed you
Immersed in your energy
I walk the path of ancestors
Called by some deep source
To your land of mystical dances
of two cultures blended.

Inhaling deeply
the Mountain that now lies beneath my feet
which guides me along your streets
the energy moves up my body
and ignites my soul
to the greater Mystery
that the natives have known.

Beautiful blue door
Once standing as a tree swaying in the wind
A witness of time
Shapeshifting into a new expression
Whispers of your life
now glazed in vivid blue
the sky brought to earth
as a portal into another space.

Incan stories woven with Spanish infusion
Life of cultural blending.
Tapestry of life
In constant evolution

Stone roads
that lead inward
Downed trees
Living as blue gateways
Of life beyond
the walls of the ordinary.

Lives of many masters
Having walked these same roads
Imprinting their wisdom
With each stone
Each wall.

I am one of many
GOD manifested in form
Walking the roads of life
Through open hearts and doors.
Entering into the realm of form
Through the veil of emptiness.

Open blue door
I see through you
Stone pathway
to the garden of paradise
that lies within view
one step at a time

Do I dare explore more
Or simply stand there staring
Do I take the next step
Of journey inward
Into deeper realms
Of the Mystery.

Do I wander in
Or just wonder about it.
Do I seek to taste the Mystery
Or merely dream about it's succulence.
Invitation to the unknown
Open blue door.
Ancient stones that bring me to your presence

10.28.05   *6:37 a.m.*

29. Keep it simple sutra

Page 1- GOD is all there IS

Page 2 - There is no spot where GOD is not.

Page 3 -My life, your life, ALL of LIFE is the life of
GOD expressing uniquely, authentically.

Page 4- LOVE is all there IS.

Page 5- The illusion of separation is just a cosmic game so you
can find the Kingdom of Heaven WITHIN -there you and I
meet and realize that there is NO you or I, just GOD.

Page 6 - LOVE is the I AM which you are

Page 6 - The answer is in the prayer and is already HERE,
go back to page 4 and open your heart,

Page 7 - Have FUN. ~ GOD

I call it the "Keep It Simple Sutra" IT being Infinite TRUTH

Written to Tom Green on Facebook,   *8.14.12*

30. Waves of Blue –

As ancient waters carved the majestic landscapes of Earth, waves of energy surged through my chakras during Saturday's meditation with Shirley, cleansing my inner terrain and sculpting a new being. Layers of history, sediment on my soul from many past lives, washed away. Stagnant energy that had been suffocating my spirit was suddenly released in bursts of light in my mind's eye. Resistance melted by the healing vibrations pulsating through each chakra.

Some may have called it a kundalini moment, how that power surged through every fiber of my being awakening me. I call it a miracle to be able to sit here two weeks later and still feel the best I have felt in nine years, with hopes and dreams alive, a sense of purpose and adventure renewed, touched by the love of my dearest friends and the Gatherers.

Waves of blue light, crashing upon karmic shores. Melting lifetimes of fear and frustrations triggered by one long tear drop from my left eye. Oceans of pent up emotions flowing afterwards. Words are useless symbols of the healing I experienced.

That day began with a slow walk across the bridge with my dear soulmate Margot. She had eyed a beautiful Kuan Yin statue (the Divine Mother in China) for Shirley the day before at the metaphysical store down the road so we decided after breakfast to get it. Perfect gift. Shirley has been that for millions, in a sense. She has guided countless souls to explore these mysteries further, she opened doors within society and in the cosmos to a knew way of looking beyond the mundane, challenging us to explore our truths and heart's desire despite the obstacles from family or friends (or the media) whose minds were closed.

On the site that bears her name, she is the "Mother/teacher/feminine guide" for us all on some level. She has provided us with a sacred space to freely discuss our intuitive insights, to divulge the most incredible, paranormal experiences, to question and learn freely without judgment. This is the sign of a mother's generous spirit. Margot was right on track with that gift and line of thinking in regard to that beautiful, green Kuan Yin.

As we crossed the bridge a little yellow butterfly flickered by, a sign of my transformation to come. The bridge was my symbol of transcending the mundane and mystical, taking me across dimensions and lifetimes to this moment with my soulmate. "Walking in two worlds" has always been the way I described myself--finding that balance of both while appreciating the NOW. I still couldn't believe the experience I had at dinner Thursday night and my time with Willy. And here I was with Margot. I felt like I was in another dimension, everything surreal. I was soaking in her presence and laughter, bonding even in the silence we shared. She was the gift my soul needed, the spiritual companion I had longed for all of my life, a spirit friend brought back to me after who knows how many lifetimes. Such an ease of being with her and a divine grace in being able to share our most intimate, spiritual and out of this world thoughts without judgment, always encouraging further explorations in this world and beyond, lessons mirrored and pillars of support for each other.

As I leaned over the bridge, I saw the riverbed below which was mostly dry exposing the stones that probably had laid there for thousands of years. Cycles of change, landscapes textured by centuries of seasons just like my spirit has experienced lifetime after lifetime. Just a small trickle left of once was probably an abundant river, I wondered how many times I sat there in another life when it rushed by wildly providing sustenance for a parched soul and a sacred society. The place felt eerily familiar and quite comfortable. What stories do the stones hold, what songs do the mountains sing. Had they seen Margot and I as well as the other Gatherers before. The surrounding landscape was lush and rich, something I don't get to see often in my neighborhood in Texas. Beyond the bridge was a field of hope and to the right a row of sunflowers whose graceful stance inspired me to stand tall facing the light, soaking in the rays of the Divine.

Right past the field was a white horse who Margot fell in love with -- Pete, she named him, a handsome fella' who seemed to trust her, allowing her to get close. In between batting flies and trying to pet him, she promised him an apple on our return and I wondered if he was ticked when later he got only half, the other half within her. Or would he appreciate that shared snack, their moment of bonding. The pictures came out cute, a gentle reminder of a nice walk with a long, lost soul friend and her new horse. She was determined to bring Pete home. I laughed thinking about a horse on a plane and Margot sitting there smiling, happy with her new found friend.

We had to make the trip twice to the store since it had been closed that first time. On the second round, I saw several of the Gatherers exploring this interesting shop--John on the floor trying to find the best Lemurian seed, Katrin, Deb, Stephen, Dee, Elaine wandering the rooms looking at angels, books, etc. and I think a few others mingling around. After picking up the statue and a Lemurian seed crystal for Willy, we sat outside the store for a moment on these high chairs and table underneath some shade while a few people smoked. The question was raised about what we thought about the meditation moving to Shirley's. I was a bit worried in regard to my stamina for the meditation and driving to Shirley's and then back for Kevin's three hour seminar so I expressed my doubts that normally I would have kept to myself.

Instantly, I realized that trickster energy was trying to allow fear to seep into my joy tainting the miracle that was already occurring. I hadn't been able to sleep in two nights (either from the altitude or the energy of this sacred land or the excitement of the Gathering) and I was concerned about the waves I was feeling. One minute tired, the next energized. But overall, I was riding it well, doing fantastic and the body pains were absent. Normally I would have been recuperating in bed for a week from so much activity. The energy of Ojo and the love of Margot, Willy and my fellow Gatherers held me strong. So I don't know where this doubt came from.

I wondered out loud much to the dismay of a few if going to Shirley's was the right thing to do. They didn't know I was speaking more from fear of my health than anything else and it was my ego and not spirit doing so. This was a once in a lifetime opportunity and a gracious gesture on Shirley's part and my heart and soul knew it. Deep down I was thrilled beyond measure. To meditate with my spiritual mentor, the woman whose books validated my dreams, my beliefs, my truths was a unique, lifetime opportunity--something I could have never imagined even though I felt I had done so in other lives.

As a young Catholic schoolgirl never exposed to such metaphysical truths, it was hard to fathom where all of these memories and emotions of life on other planets, ancient civilizations, UFOs, attractions to sacred sites, etc. came from. Not a soul to talk to about it either without some kind of admonition or threat of psychiatric care (that "you're just crazy" mantra most of us have heard). At least we no longer had to fear witch burnings (I think I felt the singe of that in another life) but the anticipated judgments in some family member's minds if my truths were exposed were enough to keep me silent for years. So when *Out On A Limb* was published I knew I was no longer alone, a freak, an outsider. I think I read it around 1986-87. I knew there had to be others with my same feelings and longings and little did I know where I'd meet some of them 15 years down the road, across that little bridge to Ojo Caliente, and that I actually would be meditating with them at Shirley's home. More hungry than tired, I caught myself in midstream, cutting off that stranger in my psyche planting such useless, energy draining thoughts and dropped it immediately because I didn't want to have to explain to others the taunting of my mind from this disease. I knew that wasn't my heart mentioning those concerns. Later, before the meditation, I went to Deb to let her know where I was coming from. Tall, beautiful Deb with such a gracious heart--she said she understood and knew it wasn't from a place of disrespect but concern about my health holding up and I felt a wave of relief. I learned from those doubts how that disease suppressed my freedom and it was time to release it's stranglehold. That was the beginning of my shift.

After our walk back, Margot and I had enough time for a quick dip into one mineral spring, shower and barely get ready for the drive to Shirley's. That trickster energy testing me again. I thought I had 30 minutes to get ready. I now had five. Our departure time got moved up. Spirit was testing my patience but I hurried along, mumbling a bit, but got ready as best as I could. I wasn't about to miss the event--lousy looking hair or not.

Off we went in our caravan to the Philips 66 station which had a Pizza Hut. Not the most enlightening food to eat before a meditation but still one of my favorites and enough to balance my jittery metabolism which annoys me since I have to fuel it so often. I saw people arriving in the parking lot as I waited for my pizza to cook. Talk about time standing still--that was the longest 5 minutes. My mind does that to me, drives me crazy with worry. I didn't want to hold anybody up or miss the drive to Shirley's. Margot kept telling me to not worry because other people were still arriving. She always grounded me when I felt my emotions flittering about like that.

In the comforts of Willy's rental car I silently blessed and then scarfed down a pizza, tried to write in the rainbow card for Shirley and catch the scenery at the same time while enjoying my time with him and Margot. I knew how vital this healing meditation was, how we planned this lifetimes ago, how the subtle effects would reach out to the universe. I didn't anticipate the powerful impact it would have on me. I was soaking in the drive but preparing myself spiritually by centering my being. It also helped that my stomach was pleasantly full. I wasn't nervous just thrilled and deeply grateful. I had this eerie feeling we were repeating a journey of many lifetimes ago, the same pilgrims being guided to a sacred site for a healing meditation.

As we paraded past the security guard, each of us waving at Harris standing there pointing the way to Shirley's, we lined the road to the right and got out to a grand vista of the mountains and then proceeded to her house. I had to hurry up and finish my card, wondering if Shirley could decipher my hieroglyphic writing.

What a beautiful soul Shirley is. Gracious and loving, she tenderly greeted each of us as if she knew everyone personally--recognitions of her old class I assumed. It seemed we had graduated to this moment. It was a beautiful home with a view of the mountains that mesmerized me and Russian sage bushes against the back wall that were simply gorgeous. For some reason I thought they were lavender.

I entered respectfully knowing I was walking into her sacred space, her home, leaving the shoes outside like my lifetime in Japan and little did I know that meditation was going to leave ages of heartaches and fears, psychic dirt, at the door of my past.

As we all poured into her living room we mingled for a bit, everyone walking around, I was too excited to snack on the cookies she had waiting for us. I was very respectful and didn't' want to look around too much at what was in her home but I couldn't help but see the photos of grandkids or nieces or nephews with moonbeam smiles and the great shot of her and Jack Nicholson with their Academy Awards. What caught my eye the most were the spectacular floral arrangements she had. Breathtaking.

There was so much light in that room--some streaming in from her beautiful windows but a lot being emanated by the souls who had gathered. A second wind had kicked in for me. I was humbly grateful to be there and feeling fantastic now.

As we settled into the living room, squeezing in 38 lightworkers prepared for their spiritual task, we told Shirley about the pattern Anita saw and how we needed to sit in that formation of the triangle, the circle, the square and everyone else supporting and protecting it with love and light. This would be the symbol that brought in the energy to open the portal of light that day. Anita with the notes of her vision guided us all into position.

Sweet, sweet Anita. Another mother energy and angelic being. I cry thinking about her, not being able to say good-bye because when I knocked at her door on Sunday no one answered. She must have been napping. But the hugs and reassurance I received from her on Saturday penetrated my heart and will hold me until I see her again.

As we moved around into our positions I was glad that I was at the front of the living room with a little extra leg room and close to Shirley. I was facing in the direction of the back windows and that gorgeous mountain range--the energy felt right. Shirley was behind me to my left but her energy encompassed the room. I had no idea where North and South was. I just sat in my spot within the circle. A few people Anita saw in her vision were not present and Margot was called by Stephen and Katrin to fill one spot next to Dee. I was elated that she joined me in the circle because her spirit is strong and wise--my dearest soul sister. Stephen was in front of me, MJ to my right, Dee to my left, Anita behind me. Such wonderful lightbeings surrounding me. The pattern was secured.

Shirley talked with us for a bit and even passed around her two necklaces--the one from the Camino and another one where I don't know where it came from but is that triangle symbol often seen with UFOs. Each one of us held them, blessed them and passed them on. The triangle surged with energy for me, I felt the pulsations and power resonating within me. The cross from the Camino was a more mellow sensation but still beautiful.

Sitting in Shirley's living room on that lush, white carpet, I felt like a student again in the ancient temples of Lemuria. Answering questions, offering opinions and thanks, listening to the others around me. I was at such peace and waves of happiness and familiarity rolled through me. This was such an honor. The room glowed with love. When she was ready, we turned around to our positions, closed our eyes and she began the meditation with a waterfall CD in the background.

At the beginning, Terry her dog was busy checking every one out. I felt a breeze as if someone was passing by to my left. I was certain it was Shirley kicking out poor Terry. As we traversed each chakra area I felt waves of energy surging within me and flashes of brilliant white light, nothing I have ever seen before, cascading through my mind's eye. Each color she called out swirled through my mind in a mysterious flow, like an elegant dancer gracefully swaying to mystical music, each layer of resistance in me dissipating. I saw images of who I needed to work with (Margot was prominent---she's always inspiring me to write---such a brilliant mentor), what I need to do in regard to my life path (spiritual films and TV shows, writing, creating a holistic center), where I need to be next (Santa Fe) and what I needed to release (lifetimes of fear and resistance so I may speak my truth freely and fearlessly and inspire people and instill hope in them).

Shirley skipped over the heart chakra and I wondered if anyone else noticed that. Meanwhile, little twinges in my left leg began to distract me, an annoyance in every meditation I do. It felt so heavy. Why the left leg, I don't know. But afterwards, instead of being dead asleep like it usually is, I just shook it a bit, stretched and was fine.

As Shirley moved up the chakras, cleansing and calling us to see our visions for each energy center, she reached the throat chakra. As the blue swirled in my mind's eye a sudden rush of emotion overwhelmed me. I tried to take a deep breath without gasping too loudly. My heart area was quickly expanding and rushing energy up to my throat. Wave upon wave of intense emotions swirled through that center. Suddenly, one big tear drop rolled down my left cheek and it took every ounce of concentration to not burst out crying.

I settled back into Shirley's soothing voice, watching this white light expanding up to my crown chakra, swirling in the tiny universes within my body and out into the immense one in the sky and in other dimensions. I have never felt such power running through my veins and spirit. Changes were occurring on a cellular and soul level, I could feel it. I felt like I was floating.

For some reason, a tiny frog popped into my mind's eye and disappeared. Then a strange image of the many faces of spiritual leaders throughout the ages transposing each other appeared, --Krishna, Buddha, Jesus, Mother Mary, Kuan Yin and others I didn't recognize. A serene Asian face kept appearing to me, a sweet smile on this androgynous being. I saw this as my path of honoring and respecting each spiritual tradition and seeking that Golden thread that connects us all, something I'd like to write about or do documentaries on while traveling the world. I have always felt the calling to unite the traditions into a path of peace, by honoring the perennial wisdom of each, by spreading a consciousness of unity in diversity, by seeing beyond the labels and rituals but focusing on the love and compassion taught in each path and how each serves a different flavor of the nectar of the Divine.

When Shirley cleansed the chakras and opened our heart one at the end, I felt such an intense release of energy, a lightness of being. I knew I wasn't the same person. Stagnant energy had been evaporated, karma transmuted and all I felt was unconditional love surging through me.

She gently brought our attention back to the room, asked us to slowly wake up and I got up after slightly stretching, not really saying anything to anyone and left through the front door and sat on the steps to the right that led to the back area which faced the mountains. Tears came rushing through, like the river flowing furiously after a spring storm. Cleansing, cleansing, cleansing-- every fear, every past life frustration, every shadow that has haunted me washed away in those tears.

I knew in that throat chakra opening that I had so much to communicate to my family and to the world. Too many secrets resided within me there, stagnating and clogging that chakra, silencing me for centuries.

Instantly, I knew that I could no longer hide from my authentic nature. I could no longer play the games of being in the closet for the sake of not being judged by my very Catholic family. I am gay, get over it. Look at my spirit and not my orientation. I am also a mystical seeker, a peacemaker, an explorer of God's multidimensional domains. I cannot conform to their religious beliefs or social conditioning. I am so happy the way I am and I can no longer cater to their images, projections, attitudes or expectations of me. It was time to come clean as my body and spirit had just experienced and to honor my path. Slowly, but surely. But I knew life was never going to be the same for me.

As the tears cleansed my essence, Jordie came out while I was sitting there and walked up next to me. I mumbled something about how healing that was and smiled. Her sweet spirit and gentleness soothed me as well as her loving hug. More people slowly poured outside. I can't remember if I did this before or after I saw Anita but I asked Willy for the keys to the car so I could get my camera. As I walked I drenched the landscape with more tears. I leaned against the car and inhaled the majestic energy of the mountains asking them to guide me so I may stand firm and strong as they do, bearing witness to my truths as they have to the history of the land.

When I came back in I went in to see Anita. Leaning into her, I buried my face into her shoulder crying and she said, "You are going to tell them, aren't you?" She knew what had happened, a major shift, a deep healing, energy surging through every fiber of my being. She said she had felt the power of the energy flowing through me. A sauna for my soul--emotional toxins from lifetimes oozing out of my being. I loved her so deeply in that moment for understanding me instantly, for providing me with that safe energy to just be me, for that tender hug that I had always wanted from my mother when I finally tell her the truth of one aspect of my being but now knowing I really don't need that approval.

I have always had a closed throat chakra (lump in my throat) even though I am very outspoken (a loud/gregarious Italian/Latin blend). That must be from my Gemini Moon--open and carefree with my friends, closed and guarded with my family--emotions that sway like the tides. The suppression of my creativity based on fear of criticism also took a toll on my body, mind and spirit. Lifetimes of repercussions for speaking up to my truths had been suffocating my current expression.

Eleven years ago, I had a stunning past life recall of being a monk during the genesis of the Nichiren Shoshu Buddhism sect, my hands tied behind my back and being beheaded. I had that flashback during my first meeting while everyone was chanting Nam-Myoho-Renge-Kyo, a familiar mantra that I had never encountered in this lifetime but it resonated within me the moment I heard it. That scene shocked me back into the reality of the meeting. I later found out the early sect leaders had literally lost their heads in the exact manner I had seen and felt. Major throat chakra trauma there.

Other memories were buried deep within my chakras reflecting that inward journey where I feared my truths and hid from my nature for the sake of conforming and being loved and literally hanging on to my dear life. So I withhold information, dance around my truths, disclose bits and pieces that are convenient to me and those energy games produced blockages in my body. I no longer feel that. Over the years I have opened up to my family about my metaphysical beliefs, my Buddhist practice----trusting in my truths-- but I still had this one big door to deal with.

I haven't come out yet but am fully prepared mentally to do so--no more fears of being ostracized, no more concerns of their Catholic oriented guilt or judgments, no more dishonoring of my spirit. It won't be as harsh now since I have interjected this dialogue about gays into their mind. They are more open and understanding. True progress thanks to my patience and persistence and low key approach of dispelling the myths and false

135

generalizations as taught by the Church or society. The minute I move out and am on my own again (which I feel will be very soon), the truth will be told. I am ready.

Another door that was opened was the honesty about this entire trip. My family thought I was meeting old friends from Los Angeles instead of past life buddies from Lemuria or some other sacred society. So I told them the truth and it was so freeing, the words flowing furiously from my excitement of having returned from this life altering trip, unhindered by their reactions, my body and mind not caring if they thought I was nuts. It was such a relief to be me and to tell them where I met the people that I love---online at Shirley's place. It took every ounce of my being not to blurt out, "Oh, by the way, been lying to you too for 17 years, I am gay! Deal with it!!" I didn't want to shock them too much but I did feel empowered.

I am preparing for part time work, a miracle after a 9 year journey with a debilitating illness ((a great teacher). The energy of Ojo, the love of Margot and Willy and all others who touched my spirit that weekend, the power of that chakra cleansing--all of it had a profound effect on me. To be so happy, with hope running freely, doubts dissolved, confidence returned, a new life emerging for the next half of my life is absolute freedom.

I am in awe of all that happened to me and indebted to the Divine for this mystical experience. Thank you from the bottom of my heart and soul. As I walked that bridge with Margot that morning, I didn't realize I would cross it later as a new woman. Side by side with my soulmate and little brother, this journey was a magical one for me. My path is enhanced by being with people who honor my spirit unconditionally, who love me wholly, who will never leave me standing on the road alone because of who I am or what I believe, who have been there for many lifetimes and will always find me.

The unconditional love of the universe, of our Mother/Father/God was coursing through my body that afternoon--both physical and astral--birthing a new me, giving me a new lease on life, a greater sense of clarity, a deeper sense of peace, and so much new love in my life that carries me forward daily with absolute hope and optimism and with a deep gratitude of the gifts of each moment in this unique incarnation. I've made other promises I need to keep, I have a calling to fulfill.

May the peace and love I have felt since that afternoon encompass the world, shine out beyond the distant galaxies, reverberate through multi-dimensions and awaken those who slumber in the mundane while missing out on the deliciousness of the mysterious and mystical nature of life.

I am still floating on that Ojo energy high!! Bowing in deep gratitude to all of my lightbeing family members, to my spirit guides, to the ancient energies and teachers of Ojo Caliente/Santa Fe but especially to my dearest Margot and brother Willy.

Meditation with Shirley MacLaine in Santa Fe, NM with The Gathering at Ojo Caliente

31. Loving Life

I was just outside holding council with the crescent moon and crickets beneath the Pecan tree who was the scribe of our heart songs. Meditating in the midst of such gorgeous incarnations brings me in touch with the ONE. I can taste the LIGHT in those subtle moments of RECOGNITION. I feel it within every fiber of my being. For indeed, GOD IS ALL THERE IS. As me, through me. As LIFE, through LIFE.

After being indoors all day on a computer, like the hamster spinning madly in his wheel, my sweet little soul has to regain her energy by being immersed in nature. Whether it's my mother's garden or White Rock Lake, that I did earlier in the night, I have to get out in order to go deeper within.

Modernity has it's absolute advantages. Don't get me wrong. I love the toys of this incarnation. I love the conveniences of air conditioning and indoor plumbing. I love the softness of my bed. I love the instantaneous communication via email or Instant Messaging with my iMac where I literally reach out and touch my best friend with a keystroke kiss. I love cell phones . I love car stereo and CDs that I blare to allow me to sing my heart out. I love making breakfast taquitos on my stove in the morning. I do love it.

However......

Nature holds the keys to the kingdom within. Secrets locked in her layers. She really does. Without bragging or nagging. She is there to open me deeper into the Mystery. Not that GOD isn't the ipod. Because I do know it IS ALL GOD. But you know the feeling, watching a sunset has a different effect than watching a soap opera.

Violet tank top, dangling purple Victoria Secret bra, baggy blue shorts along with my Nikes, hair in a pony tail, off went my little almost 43 year old incarnation to my favorite stomping ground near the Bathhouse at White Rock Lake.

Driving there I watched this older gentleman in an even older car waiting for his right turn. A smile bigger than the horizon he was savoring an ice cream cone and his energy shot fireworks of such utter JOY. Life was GOOD for this guy. Rightfully so. GOD as the guy and the Vanilla cone.

I paid attention to the attitudes and facial expressions of the GOD incarnations in my field of vision--people around or passing by--and all of the devices of this 3D realm. Soaking it all in. Knowing this is a fascinating journey. SPIRIT in many variations.

Once at the lake I was immersed in the bikers and joggers, watched the tiny, white sailboats in the distance. Found a feather that I tucked in my hemp fanny pack. Ducks gathered in gossip, birds flocked on the telephone line for the last sun's hooray. I stopped in my tracks to marvel at this one bird with such elegant, extremely long V-shaped black and white tail. Exquisite. She moved to a closer pole so I could study her form. Then saw another fine, feathered couple just like that one (don't know the name) on another line above the African American couple all cuddled up on the bench beneath them. Love was definitely in the air. All sorts of shapes and sizes. Colors and textures. Hues of my human journey. Orange glow on the liquid, goddess' body, flushed faces of kissing lovers, fabulous feathered divas and their dashing suitors.

Along the way another couple, both with big hair--really funny--was having their own drama which I often say save for the big screen. Oh, humans and creatures of all sorts of emotions and energies.

I love to walk around like a camera. Zooming in and out. Capturing it in my mind as I walked the path. The fields are turning brown, a few daisies singing their last summer song. On my way back I was joyfully surprised to find tiny tomato plants growing in the fields. I don't know why that made me so happy. But the woman who walked passed me smiled at my ecstasy.

In the distance I saw a sailboat in the middle of the lake fall to it's side and all of the others circle around it to make sure the people were fine. Compassion in the midst of relaxation. A coming together of ONE MIND in ONE HEART. Humans can be so beautiful at times.

I settled on a bench far from the regular crowd and just savored it. The skyline in the distance, the different shapes of trees, the people passing by me. It was near the house that is mine but others are temporarily living in as the universe rearranges some molecules. No harm to wish so. :)

I took many deep breaths in. Touched the tree next to me. Touched my heart. Touched my soul.

I drove home in absolute bliss. The annoyances of the earlier part of my day passed through like the summer rains do. Gentle. Not harsh. Present. But not overpowering. Lingering thoughts tried to float to the surface but I skimmed them off. Feeling human and knowing I AM SPIRIT.

I came home to conversations on the phone with former classmates and friends about Community Service, caught up with a dear college buddy, reached out to my friend of 20 years who is in LA. I remembered the crescent Moon so I went out to be mesmerized by her elegant presence. I was just in such an intimate mood. Sending love through my voice and thoughts and inhaling it with my heart. To live so present is to be so fulfilled. I was definitely in my GOD-zone.

So I share. To remind you. To savor the smiles and sunsets. The people and passionate expressions of GOD in such myriad incarnations. To take the time to tell LIFE "I love you" and to love your life with every breath.

Whether it is in the frustration of modern conveniences acting whacked out at work or in the pure JOY of being bathed in a tangerine auric bath serenaded by the crickets, just go out and savor it all.

Thanks for being present to my musings. More adventures are on the way. Day by day. Breath by breath. Oh, sweet incarnation.

Love you. Don't forget to wink at the Moon especially in her elegant, sensual crescent shape. Just gorgeous.

She says the same about us.

June 29, 2006 *Email to Friends*

32. Skypainter

Sitting on the seagreen bench beneath the Pecan tree I was immersed in the power of the Presence. In the west, SPIRT painted a marmalade sky and as the light danced across the backyard it impressed itself upon my heart and illuminated my inner being.

Anthony, Bella and Macie were making pressed drawings by rubbing paper against textured places--the tree, the stepping stones, the bench--with their favorite crayons. We do that with each other with our words, pressing our feelings in our memory creating patterns that outpicture in our life. Markings of mind movement in a world of form. I watched as Anthony struggled to keep his too big shorts on while he mimicked his older sister's every move. Little do we know who watches us for guidance. Then the sun highlighted his wavy, wild hair and filled the space with softness. I felt this energy of WHOLENESS and PEACE envelope the entire backyard enveloping us in the safety and sacredness of being.

Anthony stopped in the middle of his picture and looked up seeing the orange highlight on the cloud mass above. He shouted my name, or his version of it, and stroked his hand in the air while smiling bigger than the horizon. "Are you painting me the sunset?" I lovingly asked. 'Yeppa!" he replied in such pride for his outstanding artistry. His eyes lit up with delight to bestow such a gift to his favorite aunt. Yes, indeed, I've implanted in these kids the possibility to create the colorful sky for someone they love. Skypainter. How very beautiful.

Tilting my head back after inhaling deeply that LIGHT, it penetrated my heart and expanded my being. Looking up, I observed the emergence of the flowerings of the Elm tree that precede her new canopy of leaves. Followed the trail of a cloud moving by as if in a mindfulness meditative walk about in the sky wondering about her observations of earth. I breathed deeply and exhaled gratefully. Life. Beautiful life.

These are the moments that center me. Ground me in GOD. Guide me in my daily affairs when the world seems to spin faster than my sweet soul can take.

A dark cloud was moving in with a smoky scent. I found out later that grass fires in Oklahoma were sending their smoke signals to us in Dallas. Who says we are not interconnected. If smoke reaches us from hundreds of miles away how about love, prayers and the laughter of friends on each coast penetrating my heart as my solar companion did with her sunset dance.

Suddenly bursts of cold air signaled the Arctic front moving in shapeshifting the spring like temps on a February day. The literal winds of change. Gentle and gorgeous. I asked myself to be so open with the shifts in my life, the changes in energy fields that outpicture my new way of being as I move on, move out and move up in the world of form centered in the TRUTH of SPIRIT. I stood there embracing the incoming weather pattern. As I stand her embracing the conscious repatterning of my mind and life.

The lessons of my backyard have been profound over the years. A sacred site for my soul. My journey has been enriched by painted sunsets and moments of clarity in the TRUTH that GOD truly IS ALL THERE IS. I am the skypainter of my life. With every thought I create the colors and conditions of my life, with every choice I move my being in this world. To be SPIRIT in form, the succulent, sensational body of experience, is truly a gift. How blessed. How very blessed.

Enjoy the journey of today. Each day. The sunsets and the sacred moments of a life filled with LOVE and LIGHT.

Send beautiful thoughts to Mom for her birthday. Without her generous heart I'd be half the person I am today. Today is a sacred celebration just as each moment should be. Giving thanks this morning. For LIFE. For LIGHT. For LOVE. It's ALL GOOD.

February 17, 2006 Email to Friends

33. For Those yet to come

Slivers on the precarious parts of my fingers are swollen. Evidence of working hard at the new space for the Center For Spiritual Living. I'm not much of a handy woman but I am a quick learner. Very willing. Painting and cleaning are the two tasks I know how to do but am open to acquiring new skills while thoroughly enjoying the process.

Many I have spoken with at CSL have described the same joy even in the hardest of jobs in participating in the creation of this future, sacred space. Our love, our laughter, our energy our sweat and muscles have gone into the walls, the floors, the ceilings, the windows and even the bathrooms. We are "raising a barn" which is a center for raising our consciousness. We not only do it for ourselves but for those yet to come. The call into Spirit has been sent. Come forth and you will find a new home. A place where you can be free. Free to explore your mind and emotions. Free to heal. Free to grow. Free to be loved unconditionally. Free to release into forgiveness any lingering energy of the past so you can fly in the present.

The transformation of an office building into a sanctuary is an incredible process to witness and participate in. Hundreds of hours of labor, ideas spilling forth, negotiations back and forth, the request for volunteers in order to to save money and the desire to be part of some mystical act of service is indeed an opportunity of a lifetime. The transformation of souls is even more inspirational which is what this future space promises and this work provides.

What draws groups of people together is a mystery. Only the soul knows why we gather, why we pray together, why we laugh, why we have this desire to push the envelope of our mind, repattern the thought processes of a conditioned life, infuse our being with revelations of Spirit and tools of consciousness in order to enhance ourselves and to emanate a new way of being. We voraciously take classes in order to shift, to unleash the dead weight of the lower ego who tries to drown us with doubt, regret and denial of our innate beauty, the poison ways of our past. The toxicity of a race consciousness that has been ingrained for thousands of years. The services and classes provide the tools to clean that clouded mirror of illusion allowing for the light to shine bringing forth the birth of a new, abundant, joyful life. To fly. To be free. To be whole. When one person heals, the world slowly heals. A ripple effect of peace, a balm for a troubled planet. Each of us responsible for the energy we bring to the day and the way we walk with each other. CSL offers this sacred space for healing and renewal, for transformation and transmutation. For a new birth of a more evolved being.

This is why we gather. To challenge ourselves. To lend support. To offer guidance. To join in love and laughter. To build a bridge of light for a future of joy and peace. To reveal the essence of who we are, the TRUTH of our inherent nature. To bear witness to the Divine flow as each of us through each of us. Creating a new space is not only a gift for our souls but for those who will follow. It's not just about building walls and laying down new floors. It's about building a relationship with Spirit, with the Divine, and honoring that within everyone our path crosses but especially recognizing it within.

I've painted the walls of the upstairs classrooms while listening to disco and talking to Rev. Petra and fellow CSL members. Intimate moments blended with laughter and joy and paint all over. I have swept the future offices of the Ministers as well as the hallways and stairs creating a dust-storm. I have cleaned windows with water, vinegar and newspaper and gathered recycling strewn on the floor by some of the construction men. I've dragged out trash and gotten on my knees to pick up tossed screws and nails. Many more hours are yet to come.

I've been very conscientious of my thought process as I painted or cleaned. I want to leave only imprints of love, only an infusion of light. I want to leave a blessing everywhere I go. I vented to Rev. Petra in a closet that will have to go back and be blessed by me. Transmuting the lower energy of frustration that might have stained the walls by infusing it with prayer. Higher energy always cleansing the more stagnant ones.

Being active in my church is my simple way of giving back. Even though I know the universe is abundant and that GOOD is mine too my checkbook momentarily, just temporarily, tells a different story. One that hasn't allowed me to write big donation checks, one with a comma in it as Rev. Petra once spoke about. And until then, and even if that was the case, I still want to give of my love, of my time, of my heart, of my energy to raise this barn. Because what I have received from being at CSL has been far more valuable than any monetary assignment could represent.

How do you put a price tag on freedom? How do you define in the realm of form and finances the value of these new tools, these higher consciousness ways of being? How do you appraise the unconditional love I've received since first walking into CSL. I just realized it was my two year anniversary this weekend. When I took the giant leap of leaving my Catholic conditioning and my misery and loneliness of being the metaphysical, mystical "black sheep" of the family and drove all the way across town to some tiny church with a suite number housed in an office building in Farmers Branch that I found only through my Science of the Mind magazine. I didn't know what to expect. And I'm glad I did what I did. I was greeted with such open arms and unconditional love. Grace bathed me the moment I entered the sanctuary. I immediately knew I found a new home. Since that Sunday the changes have been immense and the growth invaluable. And the continued cycle of ego wrestling Spirit, the whole point of my humanity, is made easier by the classes I take, the services I attend, the volunteer work that I do, the love that I share.

On the wall of Rev. Petra's office is evidence of our presence. Signatures of those participating in this process. Something a future resident will find. And by then, when we have grown even more, when we have acquired the finances for our own building, we will leave behind not only the painted and partitioned walls that gave us classroom space, a huge sanctuary, a bookstore, offices and areas for celebration. We will leave the sacred energy of a family, a community, that came together for a greater GOOD, for something beyond our small selves, for the sake of our human evolution, for our future, our children. We will infuse those walls with love, laughter, joy, peace and even intellectual exchanges of the process of questioning this human experience while utilizing these spiritual tools. Pushing ourselves out of the cocoon of complacency into the beautiful birth of a new being. One that can soar. One that can co-create with the Divine mystery the life we want. One that awakens to the God qualities inherent in each of us and emanate it generously.

By raising this barn I raise my consciousness. I make a promise to myself and my community to continue forward on this path. Spiraling upwards. Remembering the Presence in each moment as I experience being a unique, human incarnation of Spirit. I know without a doubt that I am a Divine Child of God, Perfect, Whole and Complete. This revelation has been through the process of cleansing the conditioned patterns of my mind and laying down new paths of affirmative prayer. These are the gifts CSL has given me. And my time, my love, my energy in building this new space is the simple gift of gratitude I give in return. I am not be a Master Electrician in this construction process. But I AM a master of my Light in the path of my life. And I honor the gift of the Divine that moves through me as me.

Center for Spiritual Living, Dallas 2005

About the Author

Veronica Valles is a writer, poet, photographer, filmmaker, licensed spiritual coach and minister for Centers for Spiritual Living. She also claims the title of "Favorite Aunt," which she considers her greatest accomplishment in life.

With a calling to carry a notepad around like John Boy from the television show of her childhood, *The Waltons*, Veronica's dream of being a word weaver began with her voracious appetite for reading. She spent her summers at the library, learning about the world from so many authors' and narrators' perspectives. She secretly desired to be an artist like those authors, and Veronica's introverted, shy side eventually gave way to an extroverted, passionate, poetic voice.

After a nine-and-a-half-year experience with a long-term illness during her thirties, her writing turned to her spiritual transformation through the teachings of Science of Mind. What was once kept within the confines of journals and private writings has now been unleashed.

She's a simple woman who cannot contain her joy of being; her heart is centered in *love*. The next chapter of her life is unfolding as she takes on motivational speaking, workshop facilitating, teaching, writing, and more responsibility as a minister for Centers for Spiritual Living. A Texas native, you'll find Veronica in the fields of White Rock Lake. She'll be in her mother's garden chasing butterflies and fireflies with her pint-sized gurus (nieces and nephews), laughing or chanting with her friends, or simply centered in her campsite along the path.

(www.veronicavalles.com)

Printed in the United States
By Bookmasters